Conflict Management and the Future of EU Foreign and Security Policy

This book analyses how the European Union (EU) has dealt with crises and conflicts, including Russia's invasion of Ukraine, Iran's nuclear dispute and Syria's civil war, to understand the peculiar nature of its role in international security. Rather than focusing on the institutional set-up of the EU's foreign and security policy, the authors look at the 'outer' world, concentrating on crises and conflicts impinging on Europe's security. They argue that the EU and its member states' policies are constrained by systemic factors such as acute geopolitical rivalries and the fragmentation of regional governance systems, as well as by multi-source internal contestation of policies across member states. Hence, building on pragmatist-informed analysis they show that the EU's actorness in international security is first and foremost constituted by interactions with its domestic and systemic context, and as such it should be understood as a 'relational power'.

This volume will be of great use to scholars and students of International Relations, European Studies, Security, Conflict and Peace Studies, and Diplomacy Studies seeking to deepen their understanding of the subject.

Riccardo Alcaro is Research Coordinator and Head of Global Actors at the Istituto Affari Internazionali (IAI) and was the Coordinator of the JOINT project carried out during 2021–2024.

Pol Bargués is Senior Fellow at the Barcelona Centre for International Affairs (CIDOB).

Trends and Perspectives in International Politics

Trends and Perspectives in International Politics is an innovative series of analytically sound, policy-relevant volumes. It offers a comprehensive exploration of international affairs, shedding light on areas such as the climate crisis, energy, migration and multilateral cooperation. It addresses these themes both at the global level as well as looking at specific world regions: among them (but not limited to), Europe and Eurasia, North Africa and the Middle East, the Transatlantic community, the Indo-Pacific as well as sub-Saharan Africa.

Trends and Perspectives in International Politics is edited by the Istituto Affari Internazionali (IAI), the Rome-based think tank founded in 1965 on the initiative of Altiero Spinelli (https://www.iai.it/en/).

The current series editor is Leo Goretti.

The Geoeconomics of Money in the Digital Age
Nicola Bilotta

The European Union's Nuclear Non-proliferation Policy
Performance and Contestation
Manuel Herrera

Conflict Management and the Future of EU Foreign and Security Policy
Relational Power Europe
Riccardo Alcaro and Pol Bargués

"A comprehensive, up-to-date and sober assessment of the EU's role as a conflict manager and the challenges it faces in a more contested world. An essential reading for those who want to understand the historical trajectory and future outlook of EU security policies."

Ana E. Juncos, *Professor of European Politics, University of Bristol, and Editor*, Journal of European Integration

"A thoughtful and inventive new framework for understanding EU responses to contemporary crises and conflicts. The notion of relational power ingenuously illuminates the interplay of external and internal changes in shaping EU foreign policies – an interplay that menaces but also sustains the Union's distinctive security impact. A subtle, original and highly valuable contribution to current EU strategic debates."

Richard Youngs, *Senior Fellow, Democracy, Conflict and Governance Program, Carnegie Europe*

"Europe and the European Union are facing a series of current challenges in a changing World Order. This highly innovative book does not just explain what these challenges are, but opens a fruitful new avenue for thinking about ways to deal with them. The book argues that Europe, and the European Union, need to be seen as relational powers. This means that they are part of an entangled world, and they are influenced both from inside Europe and from the outside. The EU thus is not a free-floating independent entity, but part of, and actor in, the changing World Order itself. Europe acts in worldwide entanglements. Thinking this way about Europe's role in the world offers both innovative explanations for new problems and novel avenues for dealing with them."

Claudia Wiesner, *Fulda University of Applied Sciences*

"Alcaro and Bargués masterfully weave the strands of years of empirical research together in an appealing theorem on the nature of the EU as a subject of international relations. Combining an outside-in perspective with the more established inside-out ones on EU foreign and security policy, they convincingly argue that the EU's international role needs to be understood in relation to the influence of other powers when tackling crisis and conflict."

Steven Blockmans, *Editor-in-Chief*, European Foreign Affairs Review

Conflict Management and the Future of EU Foreign and Security Policy

Relational Power Europe

Riccardo Alcaro and Pol Bargués

First published 2025
by Routledge
4 Park Square, Milton Park, Abingdon, Oxon OX14 4RN

and by Routledge
605 Third Avenue, New York, NY 10158

Routledge is an imprint of the Taylor & Francis Group, an informa business

The series *Trends and Perspectives in International Politics* is edited by the Istituto Affari Internazionali (IAI).

British Library Cataloguing-in-Publication Data
A catalogue record for this book is available from the British Library

ISBN: 9781032902999 (hbk)
ISBN: 9781032999906 (pbk)
ISBN: 9781003559467 (ebk)

DOI: 10.4324/9781003559467

Typeset in Times New Roman
by codeMantra

To Manuela

To Bet and Mar

Contents

Acknowledgement

This study is based on three years of research conducted within JOINT (www.jointproject.eu/), a project carried out by a consortium of 14 research centres from the EU and beyond coordinated by the Istituto Affari Internazionali of Rome which received funding from the EU's Horizon 2020 research and innovation programme under grant agreement N. 959143 (this publication reflects only the view of the authors, and the European Commission is not responsible for any use that may be made of the information it contains). We extend our gratitude to our JOINT partners, whose works we have referenced throughout the study. Special thanks go to the colleagues who took the time to contribute their insights to our own research and revise earlier drafts of this study: Luca Barana, Margherita Bianchi, Steven Blockmans, Matteo Bonomi, Victor Burguete, Ettore Greco, Kristina Kausch, Alessandro Marrone, Pol Morillas, Pernille Rieker and Nathalie Tocci. We also thank two anonymous reviewers for their constructive feedback, and Sten Rynning, who reviewed the entire project and gave useful insights for this book, as well as the editor of the series, Leo Goretti, for his excellent editorial suggestions. This publication in open access was made possible through the generous financial support of the Fondazione Compagnia di San Paolo.

Introduction

The 21st century has confronted the European Union (EU) with mounting, at times seemingly insurmountable, obstacles in the pursuit of its foreign and security policy.

Multipolarity, a concept scholars and experts had been debating for years, eventually seemed to become a tangible reality in the 2010s, with power increasingly distributed amongst multiple players globally and even more so regionally. The failure of the various 'poles' to accommodate their diverging visions of global and regional orders has given a sharp competitive turn to multipolar interactions, with geopolitics staging a dramatic return on the world's stage. The EU has been deeply impacted, sitting as it is at the centre of three concentric circles of competitive multipolarity: the closest is Europe itself, where Russia's war of conquest in Ukraine has upended what was left of the post-Cold War security system; then there is a Middle East fraught with interstate rivalries and finally the looming contest between China and the United States in the Indo-Pacific.

Great power rivalry has found fertile ground to take roots and grow in regions where the collapse or severe weakening of state authority has led to the fragmentation of political and security governance. Local conflicts have spread insecurity across borders, exacerbated migration flows and caused social and political disruptions, while also fuelling illegal trafficking of any sort and the proliferation of armed militias and extremist groups. The EU has been deeply affected by these fragmentation dynamics, which have jolted especially (albeit not only) its extended neighbourhood, from North Africa and the Middle East to the Sahel and the Horn of Africa.

In parallel to a deteriorating international security environment, the EU has gone through a period of internal turbulence, which became especially acute in the first half of the 2010s. The Eurozone

DOI: 10.4324/9781003559467-1

crisis, the dramatic surge in refugee inflows in the wake of the civil war in Syria and the United Kingdom's referendum on exiting the EU (Brexit) hit in rapid succession the foundations of intra-EU solidarity and undermined the assumption of the presumed irreversibility of European integration. The growing appeal of nationalist forces espousing Eurosceptical views has created a new source of internal contestation of EU policies across member states.

These trends have overlapped and mutually reinforced one another in dangerous spirals. Interstate rivalry has fuelled and has been fuelled by the collapse or fragmentation of regions along a circular pattern of causality. Intra-EU divides have intermingled with both systemic factors, further complicating the process of consensus-building inside the EU. Internal divisions reflect diverging priorities that EU member state governments assign to the challenges emanating from a fragmented region. At times, such priorities are rooted in nationally constructed interests, but they can also originate from politicisation processes that parties pursue exclusively for reasons of domestic expediency. Whatever its origin, intra-EU contestation has hampered conflict management efforts and indirectly reinforced fragmentation dynamics. Similarly, great powers wedge themselves into the EU's foreign policy-decision and -making processes, animating internal debates within EU states about their broader strategic alignments.

Against the backdrop of such entangled international and domestic challenges, the exact nature of EU foreign and security policy (EUFSP) remains an open question that scholars have variously engaged with for decades. European studies generally define the EU's international actorness through the lenses of the Union's institutional capacity. For all their differences, scholars mostly think of EUFSP as a product of European integration. Consequently, negative assessments of EU performance tend to focus on the Union's institutional immaturity and structural incapacity to guarantee coordinated action, whereas more positive readings appreciate the progress made by a group of 27 (previously 28) sovereign states that purposely engage in negotiation and deliberative processes in pursuit of a joined-up foreign and security policy.

One reason for which achieving cohesion in foreign policy has become so exhausting is that the remit of EUFSP has expanded. In line with the existing literature, we define EUFSP in broad terms as encompassing actions taken by EU institutions as well as the member states across a wide array of policy areas and in coordination with various external actors. Such multi-dimensionality of its structures – multi-actor, multi-sector, multi-layered – is a defining feature of EUFSP. However, we argue in favour of conceptualising it not just based on its governance structures but also, and critically, on the context in which it unfolds, that is, on elements exogenous to the institutional setup of the EU. The nature of conflicts, the influence of other powers and regional dynamics as well as the way they interact with domestic politics across member states should be brought into the picture more systematically in the attempt to articulate the EU's actorness in international security. In doing so, we build on a body of research examining the impact of external crises on the nature of the EUFSP.[1] In particular, we follow the thread initiated by some pragmatist-informed studies[2] and integrate what has been termed an "outside-in" perspective on EU action in international security with more established "inside-out" views.[3] Outside-in perspectives have been important to 'de-centre' Europe, understand it in context, that is, in history, in relation to other powers, social structures and international processes.[4] For example, decolonial studies have shown how European integration was connected with the geopolitical interest of member states in continuing exploiting their former colonies in Africa.[5] Others have drawn on outside-in perspectives to measure the influence that third countries have on EU structures, highlighting the growing institutional ties with partners as well as the greater pressure exerted by competitors.[6] In this book, the addition of the outside-in perspective is central to relating the development of foreign policy and conflict management to structural dynamics in the international system as well as domestic factors.

According to outside-in perspectives, EUFSP has increasingly been about reacting and adapting to mounting challenges, both systemic and conjunctural. So strong has the pressure of such challenges been that they have come to dominate EU thinking – and, consequently, action – in foreign and security affairs. Nowhere has this been more evident than in geographically localised crises and conflicts, whose staggering growth and increasing interconnection have turned conflict and crisis management into a defining feature of foreign policy. As Richard Youngs puts it, EUFSP has become "problem-oriented", in that it is a constant exercise at finding – often substandard – solutions to ever more intractable crises.[7]

As far as the EU's and member states' involvement in crises and conflicts is concerned, the context of EUFSP is shaped by the three factors described at the start of this introduction. The first is the growing strategic and ideological rivalry between multiple centres of power, which we refer to as *multipolar competition*. The second is the crumbling of governance across whole regions stemming from state failure or incapacity and the myriad related challenges that spring out of it, a process we refer to as *regional fragmentation*. The third factor is a bit of an outlier, as it is neither systemic nor, crucially, external to the EU: it revolves around the domestic incentives that member state governments may have not to invest political capital in EUFSP, which we broadly call *internal contestation*. We believe that adding this internal dimension to the definition of the EUFSP context is necessary because internal contestation invariably interplays with multipolar competition and regional fragmentation in shaping the policy options of EU governments. Considering all three factors together allows us to adopt a perspective which is more in line with the daily experience of European policymakers. EU and national officials are constantly expected to ponder multipolar balances, make invariably suboptimal trade-offs between diverging priorities and determine whether their action is compatible with trends in domestic politics.

We assume these contextual factors and their growing interplay to have acted for the most part as constraints on the ability of EU institutions and member states to make full use of their foreign and security policy assets. Accordingly, we posit that the intervening effect of one or more of these factors is that of limiting the global capacity of the EU, given how relevant conflict and crisis management has become in generating international influence. Hence, we claim that EUFSP towards crises and conflicts is always a function of the capacity of EU institutions and member states to contain, mitigate or overcome these negative effects. If, as Jean Monnet once said, Europe is forged in (internal) crises and is the sum of the solutions to those crises, we contend that EUFSP is equally forged in (external) crises and conflicts and is the sum of the solutions adopted to address them.

In this book, we look at how the EU and its member states dealt with crises and conflicts – including Russia's two invasions of Ukraine, Iran's nuclear dispute, Syria's civil war and others – between approximately the mid-2000s and early 2020s. We observe how the EU deployed strategies, tactics and practices to handle the pressures of an increasingly challenging context in order to contribute to the management of conflicts and crises. We then identify some constant trends that characterise the actorness of the EU in international security. Throughout our study, we assume that the EU should be seen as a *relational power*, a concept we have developed drawing from the literature on pragmatism and relationality rather than on power in International Relations (as we discuss more at length below). Accordingly, the emphasis is very much on the 'relational' nature of EUFSP, whereas the term 'power' is used, a little generously, to indicate an international actor endowed with sufficient resources to adapt to and shape a complex environment.

Our concept of relational power captures two distinct realities that are equally central to the constitution of the EU's actorness in international security, which is where our interest lies. First, EUFSP is relational because the porosity of its institutional structures allows contextual factors to significantly influence EU policymaking (as we discuss in Chapter 3). Second, EUFSP is relational because the Union and its member states handle the contextual challenges mostly by enhancing relationships between EU institutions and member states across various policy sectors and with different external players (as we discuss in Chapter 4). Thus, 'relational power Europe' describes both the EU's structural dependence on its context and its resilience to the challenges that emanate from that context.

The concept of relational power is inherently dynamic because its constituent elements, the contextual factors and the EUFSP structures are themselves subject to change. In this book, we focus on the contextual factors because the governance structures of EUFSP remained relatively stable for years and therefore offered homogenous terms of reference for our analysis. However, change is always possible, which has led us to question whether our concept of relational power would remain valid in a situation in which the governance structures of EUFSP were transformed in the face of different configurations of contextual factors. Therefore, we conclude our research with an experiment in imagining the future, or rather three futures: one in which internal contestation plunges in the face of a significant increase in multipolar competition, and the member states agree on an institutional overhaul of the EU to face the challenges emanating from it; another in which the persistence of regional fragmentation, combined with relatively manageable levels of geopolitical rivalries and intra-EU disagreements, leads member state to move forward only in small steps; and a third one in which contestation across the Union prevails, and EUFSP governance structures are hollowed out, as member states rush to bandwagon with or counterbalance against foreign powers mired in structural competition (see Chapter 5). We consider how the EU's ways of handling the contextual challenges would change in each of such scenarios and whether our concept of relational power would still hold. We believe that the value of this exercise extends beyond the academic debates about the EU's role in international security into the policy debate about possible reforms of EUFSP structures, which not just academics but also policymakers can take as a reference point.

***

The book is divided into five chapters. Chapter 1 is an account of the evolution of the official EU discourse about its role in international security. We highlight the strong – indeed constitutive! – nexus between the EU's changing self-representations as a security player and the evolving international context (but also, implicitly, the internal one). Chapter 2 locates our work within the extant literature that conceptualises EUFSP not only as the product of European integration but also as the result of the EU's engagement with contextual factors. Chapters 3 and 4 elaborate on the concept of relational power Europe. Chapter 3 explores the relationality of EUFSP as dependence on context, in that it scrutinises the three factors that we have identified as shaping EU and member states' action in situations of crisis and conflict: multipolar competition, regional fragmentation and internal contestation. Chapter 4 focuses on the resilience capacity enshrined in the relational power of the EU as it delves into the modes with which the EU and its member states contain, mitigate or overcome the contextual challenges. The goal is to substantiate our understanding of the EU as a relational power and extract from EU crisis and conflict management specific features that characterise the actorness of the EU in international security. Finally, Chapter 5 projects our understanding of the EU as a relational power into three different scenarios of evolution of EUFSP. This is important to imagine how the EU's capacity to handle the contextual factors may evolve. In the Conclusion, we wrap up our argument and make some final considerations on relational power Europe and the EU's future role in international security.

Notes

1 Desmond Dinan, Neill Nugent and William E. Paterson (eds), *The European Union in Crisis*, London, Palgrave, 2017; Marianne Riddervold, Jarle Trondal and Akasemi Newsome (eds), *The Palgrave Handbook of EU Crises*, Cham, Palgrave Macmillan, 2021.

2 Ana E. Juncos and Simon Frankel Pratt, "Pragmatist Power Europe: Resilience and Evolution in Planetary Organic Crisis", in *Cooperation and Conflict*, 22 April 2024, https://doi.org/10.1177/00108367241244958.
3 Mathieu Segers and Steven van Hecke (eds), *The Cambridge History of the European Union: Volume 1, European Integration Outside-In*, Cambridge, Cambridge University Press, 2023.
4 Stephan Keukeleire and Sharon Lecocq, "Operationalising the Decentring Agenda: Analysing European Foreign Policy in a Non-European and Post-Western World", *Cooperation and Conflict*, Vol. 53, No. 2, 2018, pp. 277–295.
5 Peo Hansen and Stefan Johnson, *Eurafrica: The Untold Story of European Integration and Colonialism*, London, Bloomsbury, 2014.
6 Sandra Lavenex and Maria-Liisa Öberg, "Third Country Influence on EU Law and Policy-Making: Setting the Scene", *Journal of Common Market Studies*, Vol. 61. No. 6, 2023, pp. 1435–1453.
7 Richard Youngs, *The European Union and Global Politics*, London, Red Globe Press, 2021, pp. 192–193.

1 The evolution of EU foreign and security policy discourse

This chapter reads the documents in which the EU has spoken of itself as an international security player to highlight the shift away from the confident, outward-looking EU of the early 2000s, committed to promoting security, prosperity and democracy abroad, towards the more prosaic characterisations of the later years. From the 2010s onward, the EU increasingly emphasised the pragmatic nature of its approach to complex conflicts and crises. More recently, it has begun to nurture a defensive, 'geopolitical' idea of its foreign and security policy and more broadly of its international action.

Our purpose is to show how the EU has understood its role in international security in response to a constantly deteriorating context. Those who see the evolution of foreign and security policy as the result of member states' (dis)integration miss an important empirical fact. It is the appreciation of challenging international and domestic contextual dynamics and the struggle to deal with them that has led the EU to tone down its lofty ambitions to sustain a liberal, multilateral and open world order and concentrate more and more on the protection of its own security. This discursive shift is in line with an 'outside-in' perspective, in which the context has decisively shaped the EU's own understanding of its foreign and security priorities. While the EU has explicitly referenced external pressures, underlying this shift is also an implicit recognition of internal constraints.

An outward-looking EU in a safe Europe

European leaders and policymakers have engaged with the development of a common foreign policy since the Maastricht Treaty transformed the European Economic Community into the larger EU in the early 1990s. Even if intergovernmental in nature, the newly

DOI: 10.4324/9781003559467-2

created Common Foreign and Security Policy (CFSP) was presented as a significant step forward in the path towards an "ever closer union". It signalled the growing ambition by EU member states to assume a role in international security commensurate with the Union's economic size.

It did not take long for reality to bite. The "hour of Europe" hailed by Luxembourg's foreign minister Jacques Poos in June 1991 lasted the little time it took EU leaders to realise they lacked the institutional, political and military wherewithal to deal with the disintegration of Yugoslavia, the greatest security concern in Europe at the time, without the direct involvement of the United States.[1]

Still, EU leaders never abandoned their ambition to make the Union an international security actor and twice upgraded its foreign and defence institutional architecture. In 1999 a European (later Common) Security and Defence Policy (CSDP) was adopted with the ostensible goal of equipping the EU with both civilian and military conflict management capacities, while also promoting industrial cooperation and integration of defence markets. Ten years later, in Lisbon, with the latest revision of the EU treaties, EU member states beefed up the overview and steering authority of the High Representative for Foreign Affairs and Security Policy, unifying the position of the Vice-President of the Commission and head of a newly established diplomatic unit, the European External Action Service (EEAS), under the same person (hence, HRVP).[2]

In parallel with these institutional changes, the EU worked on fostering a common strategic culture. The exercise involved an effort to identify the main trends in international security as well as a reflection about how the EU viewed itself in that context. The 2003 European Security Strategy (ESS) reasoned that the unprecedented degree of freedom, prosperity and security enjoyed by Europe at the time made it imperative for the EU to project security, stability and prosperity abroad.[3] Building on its own experience of integration, the EU was supposed to contribute to international peace through the strengthening of the rule of law and the promotion of liberal norms, democracy and multilateralism.[4] Throughout the 2000s, there was widespread optimism that the EU could provide a unique approach to fostering prosperity and peace abroad, even though wars and crises in the 'enlarged' Middle East – most notably the US-led interventions in Afghanistan and Iraq – and across the Mediterranean were already tempering liberal aspirations and agendas.[5]

A pragmatic EU in a contested neighbourhood

If the 1990s marked the initial strides in the development of an EU foreign and security policy, and the early 2000s were about promise and consolidation, the late 2000s and particularly the 2010s put the EU and its member states to the test, for the global context changed considerably.

In 2016, the Global Strategy for the EU's foreign and security policy (EUGS) described a world increasingly complex and contested, in which the Union was exposed to insecurity spillovers from the many conflicts and crises that beset the regions to its east and south. The EUGS put a strong emphasis on pragmatism, albeit a "principled" one.[6] This meant that EU foreign and security policy would combine a "realistic assessment of the strategic environment" with an "idealistic aspiration to advance a better world", thus adding a good dose of nuance to the normative thrust of the previous dozen years.[7] While keeping the EU committed to multilateralism, especially through cooperative crisis management and the promotion of regional governance arrangements, the EUGS scaled the ambition of norm projection down to the narrower goal of supporting resilient societies in countries experiencing extensive contestation and conflict.[8]

The idea of resilience, defined as "the ability of states and societies to reform, thus withstanding and recovering from internal and external crises", was central to a pragmatic foreign policy.[9] Although resilience had already appeared in EU documents,[10] the concept was developed more consistently both in the EUGS and the *Joint Communication on a Strategic Approach to Resilience*.[11] A resilience-based approach provided a common language to various policy fields – from development to security – and thus, on paper, the opportunity to address different dimensions of conflicts more coherently. It also represented a pivotal move away from the ambitious objectives of externally led democracy promotion and state-building towards support for bottom-up processes of gradual recovery and constant adaptability to crises.[12]

The *Integrated Approach to External Conflicts and Crises*, released in January 2018, was informed with the same thrust towards combining principles and pragmatism. It developed from the 'co-ordination mechanisms' introduced in 2003 and the 'comprehensive approach' designed in 2013. Facing multiple dimensions of conflicts and crises, the EU vowed that it would take multifaceted coordinated action "spanning the diplomatic, security, defence, financial, trade, development cooperation and humanitarian aid fields" and throughout all phases of the conflict – prevention, crisis response, stabilisation and longer-term peacebuilding (multi-phased) – in order to contribute to sustainable peace.[13] This was to be done in a "multilateral" manner, that is, in cooperation with "international and regional partners as well as civil society organisations".[14] In short, the EU sought to develop a multi-sector and multilateral approach to address conflict and its multiple effects, thereby ostensibly overcoming the limits of unilateral, supposedly quick-fix and top-down approaches to conflict resolution.[15]

The emphasis on pragmatism that characterised the EU's foreign and security policy discourse in the first half of the 2010s was a response to a world that had indeed become more "complex and contested". But there was more to it than just a call for a less idealistic and more pragmatic approach. The EU was becoming concerned more about mitigating the impact of the outside world on itself than about shaping the outside world. The EUGS began to move away from the outward orientation of the ESS to focus on the protection of the territory, citizens and democratic systems of EU countries.[16] The priority placed on achieving strategic autonomy reflected this underlying preoccupation. The term was less a defined concept than a call on the EU to reduce its vulnerability to the political exploitation of interdependencies by foreign actors.[17] The strong emphasis on the theme of protection eventually brought about a discursive shift, as "strategic autonomy" was later reformulated as strategic or even European "sovereignty".[18]

The 2003 ESS had framed the EU's position in the world according to what International Relations theorists would call a "role identity", detailing the responsibilities that the Union had taken on itself in line with its own self-image as an outward-looking multilateralist entity. Tellingly, the focus of the 2016 EUGS also strengthened the EU's "type identity", namely its nature as an intergovernmental/supranational hybrid.[19] Accordingly, the EUGS emphasised that both EU institutions and member states contributed to a multifaceted foreign and security policy, in which all policies held an internal and external dimension.[20]

The EUGS's insistence on making use of both communitarian and national assets across a variety of policy areas was also a tacit recognition that further integration – theoretically, the most efficient solution to decision- and policymaking hurdles – had no real prospect to materialise. After all, the EUGS had been negotiated during a period of severe internal turmoil in the Union, shaken in rapid succession by the Eurozone crisis (2010–2015), the surge in refugee flows (2015–2016) and the Brexit referendum in June 2016.

To be sure, the elaboration of the EUGS was a deliberate attempt to regain a degree of initiative and give direction to the EU's international action in this more volatile context. But the new foreign and security policy framework outlined in the EUGS had an unmistakable reactive character. The Union was, after all, redirecting its own resources and those of its member states towards managing the consequences of regional instability and multipolar competition rather than championing the expansion of a rules-based multilateral system.

Overall, the EU that came out of the EUGS and the Integrated Approach was a multi-actor entity whose main concern was preventing outside instability from affecting the EU rather than projecting security and prosperity abroad. EU policymakers felt that the Union was structurally more insecure, given the downward trajectory of an international system increasingly marred by the contestation of liberal values and multilateral institutions, conflict, regional instability and interstate rivalry. They also implicitly recognised that simply urging more "joined-up" action between the EU and its member states was more in line with domestic trends than calls for further institutional integration.

A geopolitical EU in a menacing world

To navigate an international environment in which geopolitics was staging a dramatic return and regions were fragmenting, EU leaders started to speak explicitly of the need for the EU to learn the "language of power".[21] In 2019, the newly appointed European Commission led by President Ursula von der Leyen began with the promise of developing a more strategic and integrated external action to protect European sovereignty.

The assumption that the Commission and the EU as a whole were to become "geopolitical" in nature was augmented by the series of shocks that jolted Europe and the world in the following years.[22] The Covid-19 pandemic eroded trust in multilateral governance, laid bare the vulnerability of global value chains and augmented the rivalry between the United States and China, whereby the need for enhancing the Union's strategic autonomy seemed more urgent.[23] The feeling was further reinforced by Russia's second, large-scale invasion of

Ukraine in February 2022. The response by the EU and its member states, which combined draconian sanctions on Moscow with arms shipments and an accession promise to Ukraine, led HRVP Josep Borrell to speak of the "geopolitical awakening" of the EU.[24] According to Borrell, the EU's reaction to Russia's war of conquest was a significant step on the way towards the EU's geopolitical maturity, which could be measured in terms of "power and [greater] capacity to act in the world".[25]

While economic, energy or security interdependencies were traditionally seen in the EU as positive for peace and common prosperity, they were now increasingly considered as pressure points, given that foreign countries could exploit the Union's dependencies for political gains. A geopolitical EU implied that nearly every foreign policy instrument was revisited in order to reduce the EU's vulnerabilities to such weaponisation of interdependences. Trade and investment, for example, were reinterpreted through "the language of economic battlefields and trade warfare".[26] Similarly, energy relations were "geopoliticised" as the EU cultivated relations with supplier countries with which it had a broad foreign policy alignment or at least no geopolitical quarrel. Global value and supply chains were re-appreciated based on their reliability rather than cost efficiency, whereby strategies of nearshoring, friendshoring and even reshoring (including through the provisions of special support to domestic companies) were considered.[27] The EU's stated goal was to develop economic and energy sovereignty and thus boost European resilience in a context of power competition and fierce struggle for resources. Even the enlargement policy was now framed less as a merit-based process aimed at reforming the candidate members than as a geopolitical lever with which the EU could stabilise its neighbourhood through expansion.[28]

The strategic documents of the 2010s, such as the EUGS and the Integrated Approach, were reinterpreted in line with a defensive, inward-looking logic. This was the clearest in the Strategic Compass, the framework for the EU's security and defence agenda for the coming years, which the Council approved in March 2022, not even a month after the start of the Russia-Ukraine war.

While multilateral action and partnerships were central to the collective management of conflicts and crises in the Integrated Approach, the Strategic Compass pivoted towards building "strategic" partnerships, that is, partnerships with countries that were either aligned with the EU's strategic goals or could in any case be relied upon for the pursuit of narrower EU interests. Concepts such as "multilateral governance" or "global governance" were nowhere to be found in the text. Also significant was that resilience only referred to "our" resilience, the resilience of member states, which needed to be bolstered to respond to diverse crises and threats.[29] The shift from a pragmatic to a geopolitical foreign policy discourse, which was primarily concerned with the protection of Europe against external threats, was justified as a response to a changing context: "A more hostile environment and wider geopolitical trends call for the EU to shoulder a greater share of responsibility for its own security".[30]

President von der Leyen boasted herself about how the EU had matured into a geopolitical actor. She stressed the collective European response to face the socio-economic consequences of Covid-19, the relentless support to Ukraine and opposition to Russia, and the acceleration of the digital and green transition in a world of fierce competition. As she grandiosely put it: "this is Europe's moment to answer the call of history".[31] Similarly, HRVP Borrell wrote that "geo-political Europe is not just a slogan but increasingly a reality".[32]

As the rhetoric of leaders became more grandiloquent, strategies and instruments were mobilised to embolden EU foreign action. The report assessing the implementation of the Strategic Compass was congratulatory of the greater EU capacity to act with speed, flexibility and boldness in complex crises and conflicts. The European Peace Facility, established in March 2021 as an off-budget instrument with the intention to provide the Union with the financial capacity to prevent conflicts,[33] build peace and strengthen international security, was depicted as "a game changer".[34] The reason for this was that the European Peace Facility was then used to support member states' deliveries of weapons to Ukraine as well as to finance a CSDP training mission there. The civilian and military dimensions of EU conflict management were consequently elevated to an unprecedented level of possibility. The geopolitical posture of the EU, according to its own discourse, had no ceiling.

Conclusion

According to its own self-constructions, the EU's role in international security shifted from multilateralist and normative to principled and pragmatic, and then towards defensive and geopolitical. This discursive repositioning, which led to prioritise the reduction of vulnerabilities emanating from interdependences with other countries and the strengthening of European resilience, was informed by a world increasingly fragmented in which power politics was running amok. This emphasis on the complex and contested international system and its interplay with EU politics, we observe, contrasts with academic perspectives that have examined and debated the EU's role and discourse according to its norms and institutional capacity. Some scholars continue to view the EU's singular contribution to international security in normative terms, looking at how it can still sustain multilateral regimes and build on the concept of resilience to further international crisis management and resolution.[35] Yet few, if any at all, are under the illusion that an EU normative foreign policy may be enough to rescue a liberal multilateral order strained by multipolar tensions and regional fragmentation.[36]

However, many scholars see merit in the "geopolitical awakening" of the EU against the backdrop of a more uncertain and hostile international environment. They see the crises as opportunities for institutional reform, applaud the EU's involvement in great power politics, as much as the commitment by member states, best exemplified by Germany's intent to significantly upgrade its military spending to face the *Zeitenwende* ("historical turning point") brought about by Russia's war against Ukraine.[37] Yet most remain sceptical that the EU may ever develop a 'geopolitical' identity and become a great power in the traditional sense of the term. While EUFSP may have acquired features of a more strategic, standard foreign policy, so the argument goes, it remains far from achieving that status. The reason is that the EU remains an incomplete political project and a deficient institutional construct. Many scholars continue to see EUFSP as a second-order instrument impaired by its largely intergovernmental character, which blocks the initiative and resourcefulness of supranational institutions and forces them to adopt at best a complementing or supervisory role.[38] Others point to the growing politicisation of foreign policy issues and instruments, which has become more common in a world where crises and conflicts abound and great power rivalry is on the rise, shrinking the room for intra-EU agreement.[39]

If neither normative nor geopolitical, what is the 'true' nature of EU foreign and security policy? We seek to answer this question and contribute to the debate by advancing the notion that the EU has become a relational power. Whereas the theories and perspectives in EU studies tend to focus primarily on the inner functioning and resources of the

EU, our conclusion drives from the observation that the EU is both permeated by and constantly reacting to a ‘shifting outside’, which then feeds back into European domestic politics. In the next chapter, we review the theories that have sought to grapple with an evolving EUFSP in order to flesh out our own contribution.

Notes

1 Josip Glaurdić, *The Hour of Europe. Western Powers and the Breakup of Yugoslavia*, New Haven/London, Yale University Press, 2011.

2 Treaty on the European Union, Art. 18 (on the HRVP), Art. 23 and ff. (on CFSP), Art. 47 and ff. (on CSDP) and Art 27.3 (on the EEAS).

3 Council of the EU, *European Security Strategy. A Secure Europe in a Better World*, Brussels, Publications Office of the EU, 2009, pp. 23 and ff., https://data.europa.eu/doi/10.2860/1402. For an analysis of the ESS’ genesis and contents, see Alyson J.K. Bailes, “The European Security Strategy. An Evolutionary History”, in *SIPRI Policy Papers*, No. 10, February 2005, https://www.sipri.org/node/1631.

4 Karen E. Smith, *European Union Foreign Policy in a Changing World*, Cambridge, Polity Press, 2003.

5 Federica Bicchi, “‘Our Size Fits All’: Normative Power Europe and the Mediterranean”, *Journal of European Public Policy*, Vol. 13, No. 2, 2006, pp. 286–303, https://doi.org/10.1080/13501760500451733. See also, Michelle Pace, Peter Seeberg and Francesco Cavatorta, “The EU’s Democratization Agenda in the Mediterranean: A Critical Inside-Out Approach”, *Democratization*, Vol. 16, No. 1, 2009, pp. 3–19, https://doi.org/10.1080/13510340802575783.

6 European External Action Service (EEAS), *Shared Vision, Common Action: A Stronger Europe. A Global Strategy for the European Union’s Foreign and Security Policy*, Brussels, Publications Office of the EU, 2016, https://data.europa.eu/doi/10.2871/9875.

7 Ibid., p. 16. See also Ana E. Juncos, “Resilience as the New EU Foreign Policy Paradigm: A Pragmatist Turn?”, *European Security*, Vol. 26, No. 1, 2017, pp. 1–18, https://doi.org/10.1080/09662839.2016.1247809.

8 Nathalie Tocci, *Framing the EU Global Strategy. A Stronger Europe in a Fragile World*, Cham, Palgrave Macmillan, 2017. See also, Pol Morillas, *Strategy-Making in the EU. From Foreign and Security Policy to External Action*, Cham, Palgrave Macmillan, 2019.

9 European External Action Service (EEAS), *Shared Vision, Common Action: A Stronger Europe. A Global Strategy for the European Union’s Foreign and Security Policy*, Brussels, Publications Office of the EU, 2016, https://data.europa.eu/doi/10.2871/9875, p. 23.

10 Specifically, the Commission’s *Communication on Food Security* of 2012 and the *Resilience Action Plan 2013–2020* (see European Commission, *The EU Approach to Resilience: Learning from Food Security Crise*s (COM 2012/586), 3 October 2012, pp. 5–7, https://eur-lex.europa.eu/legal-content/

en/TXT/?uri=celex:52012DC0586; European Commission, *Action Plan for Resilience in Crisis Prone Countries 2013–2020* (SWD 2013/227), 19 June 2013, http://aei.pitt.edu/58235)

11 European Commission and EEAS, *A Strategic Approach to Resilience in the EU's External Action* (JOIN 2017/21), 7 June 2017, https://eur-lex.europa.eu/legal-content/en/TXT/?uri=celex:52017JC0021.

12 Nathalie Tocci, "Resilience and the Role of the European Union in the World", *Contemporary Security Policy*, Vol. 41, No. 2, 2020, pp. 176–194, https://doi.org/10.1080/13523260.2019.1640342.

13 Council of the EU, *Council Conclusions on the Integrated Approach to External Conflicts and Crises* (5413/18), 22 January 2018, point 1, https://data.consilium.europa.eu/doc/document/ST-5413-2018-INIT/en/pdf.

14 Ibid. See also, European External Action Service (EEAS), *Shared Vision, Common Action: A Stronger Europe. A Global Strategy for the European Union's Foreign and Security Policy*, Brussels, Publications Office of the EU, 2016, https://data.europa.eu/doi/10.2871/9875, pp. 28–29.

15 Riccardo Alcaro et al., "A Joined-Up Union, a Stronger Europe. A Conceptual Framework to Investigate EU Foreign and Security Policy in a Complex and Contested World", in *JOINT Research Papers*, No. 8, March 2022, https://www.jointproject.eu/?p=969.

16 Ibid.

17 Mark Leonard, *The Age of Unpeace. How Connectivity Causes Conflict*, London, Penguin Random House/Bantam, 2021.

18 On strategic or European sovereignty, see amongst others Suzana Anghel, "Strategic Sovereignty for Europe", in *EPRS Briefings*, September 2020, https://www.europarl.europa.eu/thinktank/en/document/EPRS_BRI(2020)652069; for an analysis of the genesis and content of this concept, see Bruno Dupré, "European Sovereignty, Strategic Autonomy, Europe as a Power: What Reality for the European Union and for What Future?", in *Schuman Papers*, No. 620, 25 January 2022, https://www.robert-schuman.eu/en/european-issues/0620.

19 Alexander Wendt, *Social Theory of International Politics*, Cambridge, Cambridge University Press, 1999, p. 198.

20 Christopher Hill, "Convergence, Divergence and Dialectics: National Foreign Policies and the CFSP", in Jan Zielonka (ed.), in *Paradoxes of European Foreign Policy*, The Hague, Kluwer Law International, 1998, pp. 35–51. See also, Karen E. Smith, *European Union Foreign Policy in a Changing World*, Cambridge, Polity Press, 2003; and especially Ben Tonra and Thomas Christiansen (eds), *Rethinking European Union Foreign Policy*, Manchester, Manchester University Press, 2004.

21 Josep Borrell, "Embracing Europe's Power", in *Project Syndicate*, 8 February 2020, https://prosyn.org/UZNbi12.

22 Von der Leyen herself referred to the Commission she led as "geopolitical". See European Commission, *Speech by President-elect von der Leyen in the European Parliament Plenary on the Occasion of the Presentation of Her College of Commissioners and Their Programme*, 27 November 2019, https://ec.europa.eu/commission/presscorner/detail/en/speech_19_6408. For an analysis, see Pierre Haroche, "A 'Geopolitical Commission':

Supranationalism Meets Global Power Competition", *Journal of Common Market Studies*, Vol. 61, No. 4, July 2023, pp. 970–987, https://doi.org/10.1111/jcms.13440.

23 Riccardo Alcaro and Nathalie Tocci, "Navigating a Covid World: The European Union's Internal Rebirth and External Quest", *The International Spectator*, Vol. 56, No. 2, June 2021, pp. 1–18, https://doi.org/10.1080/03932729.2021.1911128. See also Tara Varma, "European Strategic Autonomy: The Path to a Geopolitical Europe", *The Washington Quarterly*, Vol. 47, No. 1, 2024, pp. 65–83, https://doi.org/10.1080/0163660X.2024.2327820, https://twq.elliott.gwu.edu/files/2024/04/Varma_TWQ_47-1-e17d9c2d2dd81a76.pdf.

24 Josep Borrell, "Europe in the Interregnum: Our Geopolitical Awakening after Ukraine", in *Géopolitique*, 24 March 2022, https://geopolitique.eu/en/?p=10796.

25 EEAS, *Geopolitical Europe: Speech by High Representative/Vice-President at the EP Plenary*, 18 October 2023, https://www.eeas.europa.eu/node/434503_en [translated by authors].

26 Sophie Meunier and Kalypso Nicolaidis, "The Geopoliticization of European Trade and Investment Policy", *Journal of Common Market Studies*, Vol. 57, Annual Review, September 2019, pp. 103–113 at p. 103, https://doi.org/10.1111/jcms.12932.

27 Anna Herranz-Surralles, "The EU Energy Transition in a Geopoliticizing World", in *Geopolitics*, 2 January 2024, Vol. 29, No. 5, pp. 1882–1912, https://doi.org/10.1080/14650045.2023.2283489.

28 Frank Schimmelfennig, "The Advent of Geopolitical Enlargement and Its Credibility Dilemma", in Jelena Džankić, Simonida Kacarska and Soeren Keil (eds), *A Year Later. War in Ukraine and Western Balkan (Geo)Politics*, Brussels, Publications Office of the EU, 2023, pp. 185–193, https://data.europa.eu/doi/10.2870/275946.

29 Pol Bargués, "From 'Resilience' to Strategic Autonomy: A Shift in the Implementation of the Global Strategy?", in *EU-LISTCO Policy Papers*, No. 9, February 2021, https://zenodo.org/doi/10.5281/zenodo.4548132.

30 Council of the EU, *A Strategic Compass for Security and Defence*, 14 March 2022, p. 13, https://www.eeas.europa.eu/node/410976_en.

31 European Commission, *State of the Union 2023*, 13 September 2023, https://ec.europa.eu/commission/presscorner/detail/en/speech_23_4426.

32 EEAS, *Annual Progress Report on the Implementation of the Strategic Compass for Security and Defence*, March 2023, p. 4, https://www.eeas.europa.eu/node/426781_en.

33 Council of the EU, *Council Decision (CFSP) 2021/509 of 22 March 2021 Establishing a European Peace Facility*, http://data.europa.eu/eli/dec/2021/509/2024-03-18.

34 EEAS, *Annual Progress Report on the Implementation of the Strategic Compass for Security and Defence*, March 2023, p. 8, https://www.eeas.europa.eu/node/426781_en.

35 Eric Stollenwerk, Tanja A. Börzel and Thomas Risse, "Theorizing Resilience-Building in the EU's Neighbourhood: Introduction to the Special Issue", *Democratization*, Vol. 28, No. 7, 2021, pp. 1219–1238, https://doi.org/10.1080/13510347.2021.1957839; Nathalie Tocci, "Resilience and the

Role of the European Union in the World", in *Contemporary Security Policy*, Vol. 41, No. 2, 2020, pp. 176–194, https://doi.org/10.1080/13523260.2019.1640342.

36 Pol Bargués, Jonathan Joseph and Ana E. Juncos, "Rescuing the Liberal International Order: Crisis, Resilience and EU Security Policy", *International Affairs*, Vol. 99, No. 6, November 2023, pp. 2281–2299, https://doi.org/10.1093/ia/iiad222. See also, Leonard Schuette and Hylke Dijkstra, "The Show Must Go On: The EU's Quest to Sustain Multilateral Institutions since 2016", *Journal of Common Market Studies*, Vol. 61, No. 5, September 2023, pp. 1318–1336, https://doi.org/10.1111/jcms.13466.

37 Mark Leonard, "The European Union as a War Project. Five Pathways toward a Geopolitical Europe", in Hal Brands (ed.), *War in Ukraine. Conflict, Strategy, and the Return of a Fractured World*, Baltimore, Johns Hopkins University Press, 2024, pp. 258–272, https://muse.jhu.edu/pub/1/oa_edited_volume/chapter/3881930; Calle Håkansson, "The Ukraine War and the Emergence of the European Commission as a Geopolitical Actor", *Journal of European Integration*, Vol. 46, No. 1, 2024, pp. 25–45, https://doi.org/10.1080/07036337.2023.2239998. See also, Daniel Fiott, "In Every Crisis an Opportunity? European Union Integration in Defence and the War on Ukraine", *Journal of European Integration*, Vol. 45, No. 3, 2023, pp. 447–462, https://doi.org/10.1080/07036337.2023.2183395; Mitchell A. Orenstein, "The European Union's Transformation after Russia's Attack on Ukraine", *Journal of European Integration*, Vol. 45, No. 3, 2023, pp. 333–342, https://doi.org/10.1080/07036337.2023.2183393; Sven Biscop, "No Peace from Corona: Defining EU Strategy for the 2020s", *Journal of European Integration*, Vol. 42, No. 8, 2020, pp. 1009–1023, https://doi.org/10.1080/07036337.2020.1852230.

38 Heidi Maurer and Nicholas Wright, "Still Governing in the Shadows? Member States and the Political and Security Committee in the Post-Lisbon EU Foreign Policy Architecture", *Journal of Common Market Studies*, Vol. 59, No. 4, July 2021, pp. 856–872, https://doi.org/10.1111/jcms.13134. See also, Sandrino Smeets, Alenka Jaschke and Derek Beach, "The Role of the EU Institutions in Establishing the European Stability Mechanism: Institutional Leadership under a Veil of Intergovernmentalism", *Journal of Common Market Studies*, Vol. 57, No. 4, July 2019, pp. 675–691, https://doi.org/10.1111/jcms.12842.

39 Esther Barbé and Pol Morillas, "The EU Global Strategy: The Dynamics of a More Politicized and Politically Integrated Foreign Policy", *Cambridge Review of International Affairs*, Vol. 32, No. 6, 2019, pp. 753–770, https://doi.org/10.1080/09557571.2019.1588227. See also, David Cadier and Christian Lequesne, "How Populism Impacts EU Foreign Policy", in *EU-LISTCO Policy Papers*, No. 8, November 2020, https://zenodo.org/doi/10.5281/zenodo.4282192; Katja Biedenkopf, Oriol Costa and Magdalena Góra, "Introduction: Shades of Contestation and Politicisation of CFSP", *European Security*, Vol. 30, No. 3, 2021, pp. 325–343, https://doi.org/10.1080/09662839.2021.1964473; Richard Youngs, "EU Foreign Policy and Energy Strategy: Bounded Contestation", *Journal of European Integration*, Vol. 42, No. 1, 2020, pp. 147–162, https://doi.org/10.1080/07036337.2019.1708345; Patrick Müller and David Gazsi, "Populist

Capture of Foreign Policy Institutions: The Orbán Government and the De-Europeanization of Hungarian Foreign Policy", *Journal of Common Market Studies,* Vol. 61, No. 2, March 2023, pp. 397–415, https://doi.org/10.1111/jcms.13377.

2 Inside-out theories of EU foreign and security policy

The integration drive on which EU countries embarked throughout the 1990s and early 2000s provided the background for continual academic debates about the transformations that the Union was experiencing. While foreign and security policy had remained largely outside of the integration thrust, scholars increasingly took an interest in it too. The underlying reasoning was that an economically more integrated EU would inevitably shape the member states' appreciation of their collective international role. Besides, as we have seen in Chapter 1, EU member states themselves were making bold statements about advancing cooperation in matters of security and defence, exemplified by the creation over the years of the CFSP and CSDP, the HRVP and EEAS, as well as numerous instruments such as the Permanent Structured Cooperation or the European Peace Facility.

In this chapter, we review two academic debates that have shaped the general understanding of EUFSP. The first addresses the question of the extent to which the drivers of European integration (alternatively, member states, supranational institutions, issues of identity or a combination of all these factors) justify the proposition that the EU has a distinctive actorness in international security. The second debate deals with the kind of power that the EU holds or, better, is – whether it is a civilian, a normative, a military power or a different kind of power. While perspectives differ and have clashed over the years, we suggest that they share a similar 'inside-out' angle when responding to these questions, namely a strong focus on the EU's inner functioning.

Theoretical accounts of EU foreign and security policy

As the EU moved forward in its various integration leaps during the 1990s, intergovernmentalism emerged as a major theory of

DOI: 10.4324/9781003559467-3

explanation of the process. In Andrew Moravcsik's liberal version of intergovernmentalism, European integration is the result of a bargain between governments acting upon domestically produced national preferences. European institutions, therefore, "can be analysed as a successful intergovernmental regime designed to manage economic interdependence through negotiated policy co-ordination".[1] Within this framework, European institutions are outcomes rather than actors, and therefore structurally incapable of driving integration forward. Only member states can.

This intergovernmental logic was seen to dominate EU policymaking, especially in foreign and security policy, where domestic constituencies favouring supranational integration have never managed to tilt the balance in their favour. This is also the position of later forms of intergovernmentalism, including non-rationalist, 'deliberative' accounts of it.[2] Intergovernmentalists see the institutional outcome in the foreign and security policy field as structurally coordinated policy, equipped with staff and resources but still firmly under national control.[3] As such, EU foreign and security policy remains that segment of national foreign policy that European states share with their fellow EU members. In other words, according to liberal intergovernmentalists, the EU is not so much an international security actor per se as an instrument amplifying the influence of the member states.

This conclusion is not far from that held by the realist branch of intergovernmentalism, whose adherents also participated in the debate, particularly as Europe's geopolitical landscape darkened from the late 2000s onwards. While emphasising power relations – notably between France and Germany – rather than economic interdependence as the main rationale for EU integration, they see the process as state-driven and state-controlled, much as liberal intergovernmentalists do.[4] In their view, the EU is a security system that has embedded German continental hegemony in a stable (institutionalised) set of cooperative relations with its fellow EU members, especially France, with whom Germany shares hegemonic responsibilities.[5] EU foreign and security policy is consequently mostly viewed as a platform amplifying French and German power.

Intergovernmentalism's narrow focus on member states' preferences and their underlying domestic societal pressures or power asymmetries has historically met with criticisms.[6] Neofunctionalists have continued to emphasise the role of supranational institutions and in particular the entrepreneurship capacity accruing to EU officials from their technical expertise in handling member states' interdependencies.[7] Neofunctionalist scholars have pointed to the greater powers and resources with which the Lisbon Treaty endowed the Commission as well as the proactive role of the European Central Bank to shield the Eurozone from financial catastrophe in 2012 as continuous validation of the spillover effect, whereby integration in one field gradually creates a need for integration in other policy domains.[8]

Neofunctionalism is expected to explain also advances in the integration of security and defence, however limited integration has been in those areas when compared to other ones. Since Lisbon, supranational offices (HRVP) and agencies (EEAS) have helped bridge the gap between member states and have carried out a separate foreign policy.[9] Another case in point is the incremental progress made by CSDP, with the activation in the late 2010s of the Permanent Structure Cooperation and the creation of the European Defence Fund and European Peace Facility (and the use of the latter to finance EU member states' arms transfers to Ukraine). Scholars have analysed how EUFSP entrepreneurs can bring about more homogeneity in the foreign policy outlook of member states, like former HRVP Federica Mogherini did with the formulation of the EUGS.[10] Contra intergovernmentalism, neofunctionalism understands the EU as a process rather than an outcome. Supranational institutions have levers to drive forward integration or at least more EU-level cooperation. In this vein, EUFSP gains an ontological status distinct from national foreign policies, and consequently, the EU can legitimately be seen as an actor of international security.

The rationalist perspective on European integration adopted by intergovernmentalism and neofunctionalism has appeared to many scholars too narrow to understand an overly complex phenomenon that cannot be reduced to rational choice-driven decisions. Postfunctionalist theorists have excelled in explaining the limits of intergovernmentalist and neofunctionalist expectations for integration. They trace such limits to the (in)compatibility of European integration with national (or subnational) belief systems that are politicised by domestic actors.[11] They note how the success of right-wing nationalist parties in politicising migration management and of both right- and left-wing forces in doing the same with fiscal austerity has opened the door to perspectives favouring less engagement within existing EUFSP structures, differentiated integration or even disintegration.[12]

Postfunctionalists put the premium on mass politics and public opinion and perceptions, rather than rational and interest-seeking elites. For the most part, postfunctionalists have underlined the negative aspects of identity politics, highlighting the exclusivist nature of nationalist or sovereignist narratives brought in by far-right and other populist parties and how these have impacted on norms and practices of EU integration and indirectly on foreign and security policy.[13] However, other studies have shown how questions of identity can also deepen European integration.[14] Despite the consolidation of populism across Europe, these scholars see a rich process of European socialisation, in which transnational interactions have grown constantly alongside the building of collective identities.[15] Complementing postfunctionalist perspectives, constructivist scholars have long emphasised how EU membership involves the voluntary acceptance of a specific political order and the related set of norms, rules and behavioural codes, regardless of their formally binding nature.[16] This entails ideas, narratives and policymaking practices that shape interests and enrich the relationship between member states and the EU.

This logic easily extends to foreign policy, in that member states construct their international interests through their interaction with the EU. This is the base for what some call a "collective European responsibility to act", which has endured for decades as a constant foreign policy driver.[17] The multifaceted and joined-up response to Russia's invasion of Ukraine put up by EU institutions and member states may be seen, from this perspective, as the culmination of this. Insofar as constructivists conceptualise the EU as a two-way street process of reciprocal constitution between common institutions and member states, the EU is construed as a multi-actor entity and an established international security player.

These various theoretical perspectives disagree on the drivers and facets of EU (dis)integration and the nature of EUFSP, yet they also have something in common. They all share an inside-out perspective.[18] In mainly analysing the relationship between EU institutions and member states – especially the formal and informal obligations that have fostered ever more routinised, if not institutionalised, forms of cooperation – they conceptualise EUFSP as the result of the EU's values and institutional structure.[19] Even in more recent attempts to revisit these theories in the light of the crises of the 2010s – from the Eurozone crisis to Brexit and the rise of illiberal democracy – international affairs are largely kept outside of the matrix.[20] This is critical since these inside-out perspectives have informed studies that seek to capture the special nature of the EU as an international security actor, which we consider in the next section.

Theoretical constructions of the EU's 'power'

The European Economic Community acquired greater international presence and furthered international economic relations and cooperation in the early 1970s, profiting from a temporary but significant phase of détente between the Cold War rival blocs. At the time, François Duchêne famously described the Community as a "civilian power" that was developing "civilian forms of influence and action" and could become "the exemplar of a new stage in political civilisation".[21] Over the years, studies have shown how the EU's apparent weakness – the lack of military power – compelled it to develop other ways to influence international affairs such as diplomacy, regulation and economic interdependence. For example, Moravcsik applied its liberal understanding of power to argue that Europe's diplomatic, financial, technological and military resources, amplified by institutionalised policy coordination, were considerable enough to qualify it as a superpower (though a "quiet" one given the EU's intrinsic reluctance – or inability – to play power politics).[22] Other more recent reiterations of the EU as a civilian power, such as the depiction of the EU as a "regulatory" power or a "market power", draw on a (neo)functionalist perspective. They argue that the EU's supranational institutions and market-driven policies have a decisive influence abroad, prompting alignment with the rules, standards and regulations governing the single market.[23]

Nevertheless, the notion that power may be exerted without a strong and autonomous military capacity has long been contested. "'Europe' is not an actor in international affairs, and does not seem likely to become one", is the (in)famous sentence with which Hedley Bull dismissed the Community's international aspirations back in 1982.[24] The English School theorist challenged the idea that Europe was a civilian power (a prevalent view at the time following Duchêne's analysis). He argued that the European Community would only be a power if it acquired military capabilities and a nuclear deterrent, so as to free itself of its dependence on the United States.[25] Similarly, classical realists argued that the European Community was only a vehicle for cooperation "on a limited range of second-order issues"; this was made possible by the stalemate induced by bipolarity and with the United States role as security provider.[26]

Since the end of the Cold War, and particularly after the inception of CFSP and CSDP, the perception that the EU was a security power has grown, although its minimal military capabilities continue to perplex theorists.[27] Classical realist arguments inform the view of those who define the EU as a "small" power, whose culture and institutional architecture constrain the development of strategic actorness; in the field of security, they assume that the EU is a subsystem of a larger Euro-Atlantic order whose centre of gravity lies across the ocean.[28]

In addition to conceptualisations that only focused on the military/civilian divide, in the early 2000s Ian Manners famously theorised about the EU as a "normative power". He argued that the EU had "the ability to define what passes for 'normal' in world politics" through the diffusion of norms developing inside Europe such as the transnational parliament, democratic conditionality and human rights, thereby transforming international affairs.[29] The notion of normative power Europe always met fierce resistance. Realist authors saw it as idealistic, detached from the true intentions of European countries and the crude realities of interstate competition.[30] Studies saw potential but also evident limitations in the implementation of value-driven policies.[31] In particular, the idea of normative power Europe was criticised when evaluating the EU's democracy promotion and state-building interventions in conflict-affected societies such as the Western Balkans or in the context of the Arab uprisings in 2011. The EU was accused of acting as a "normative empire" willing to impose norms on other countries.[32] Other scholars focused on the institutional limitations of the EU, which for example hindered its capacity to become a "normative gender actor".[33]

Still, this conception was influential to define the purpose of EUFSP, which was meant to be driven by the promotion of ideas and values, rather than political, economic or military interests. Nathalie Tocci's recent depiction of Europe as a "global and green" player, whose new *raison d'être* is to enable the energy transition, has its roots in the way constructivists view the relationship between EU institutions and member states as an intersubjective identity-shaping process.[34] Without the EU's normative framework, Tocci would contend, it would be hard to imagine the member states claim a leadership role in global climate and energy politics.

Research on the EU's distinctive power, as much as debates and polemics around the civilian, military or normative nature of it, continue to this day. What is interesting for our argument is that, while different, these constructions of Europe start from the internal resources as well as values and institutional structures of the EU to describe its distinctive actorness in international affairs.[35] In this book, we take a different road.

Relational power Europe

In recent years, a group of scholars have adopted an outside-in perspective in the attempt to capture what inside-out views miss, which is the way the EU's policymaking processes are affected by factors external to the institutional set-up of the Union itself. Sandra Lavenex and Marja Liisa Öberg, for instance, have argued that the intensification and deepening of institutional arrangements between the EU and a number of variously associated countries (involved in the enlargement process, the neighbourhood policy and other contractual-based arrangements) warrant "a step in the study of EU external relations from the inside-out to the outside-in perspective".[36] While they deliberately limit their focus to these countries, they recognise that other external factors may be equally relevant in shaping EU foreign policymaking.[37] Outside-in perspectives have been central to contextualise Europe alongside other powers, cultures and histories, acknowledging the agency of the rest and a more complex configuration of the global order.[38] In our study, this is important because EU efforts of conflict-management today cannot be understood without the study of systemic trends such as multipolar competition and regional fragmentation. We integrate an outside-in perspective with an inside-out one because systemic factors often interplay with one another as well as with the increasingly contested politics of the EU in shaping EU foreign policymaking processes.

In our view, the merit of this approach is to trace the EU's international actorness to the *interaction* between the internal dynamics highlighted by the inside-out perspectives and external, systemic ones. Along those lines, pragmatism-informed studies of EUFSP have theorised an EU whose power resides in its ability to adapt to crises and shocks in multiple ways.[39] Neither (just) values nor (only) crude *Realpolitik* drive EUFSP, according to pragmatists. Instead, the EU is seen to muddle through international affairs by integrating a number of normative, political and strategic (security and economic) concerns that evolve over time; this makes its foreign policy fundamentally adaptable and pragmatist.[40]

The EU's power is in this perspective not so much the upshot of its military, civilian or other capabilities; instead, it lies in the dense interactions among European actors, and between these and external players while responding and adjusting to diverse challenges.[41] Ana Juncos and Simon Pratt have spoken of a "pragmatist power EU", in which the EU changes its environment and partners as well as changes itself "within processes of policymaking and deliberation, to transform as an entity alongside a transforming set of planetary needs, demands and goals, including during times of unprecedented crisis".[42] Similarly, Brigid Laffan has theorised Europe as a "collective power", noticing how it is becoming an agile player that increasingly innovates and mobilises resources to act resolutely, as seen in the response to the difficulties generated by Brexit, the Covid-19 pandemic and the Russia-Ukraine war.[43] These studies have thus begun to understand the EU in relation to internal and external challenges, as an entity that is constituted and becoming through practices and their effects in a volatile context.[44] In our view, this pragmatist direction is central to grasp how the EU is evolving and addressing conflicts and crises.[45]

It is from these two strands of research – one introducing an 'outside-in' perspective and another insisting on the relationality and becoming of the EU's actorness – that we draw our concept of 'relational power Europe'. It is relevant to emphasise the theoretical roots of such concept of ours in order to distinguish it from the literature on power in International Relations. There, 'relational power' indicates the deliberate action taken by one party to compel another party into action or inaction; the 'relational' part of the phrase describes the power asymmetry between two parties.[46] In these terms, 'relational power' is opposed to 'structural power', which indicates the indirect ability of an international player to have other parties conform with its desiderata not out of a deliberate – 'relational' – action, but as a result of a structural position of dominance (mostly in security and economy, but possibly in other fields too).[47] Clearly, this is not what we mean by 'relational power Europe'. With our theoretical background being the literature on relationality, our contribution is to think of EUFSP in terms of "relational processes unfolding".[48] As we anticipated in the Introduction, we seek to capture the entwinement between the internal and external, the contextual and the institutional, to articulate the actorness of the EU in international security.

In light of the above, our concept of relational power Europe should be understood as capturing the dual nature of EU foreign and security policy. First, we claim EUFSP to be relational because its structures are porous, whereby the contextual factors find multiple avenues to impinge on EU foreign policymaking. 'Relational' here indicates a constitutive dependence on context, which is stronger than, but not too dissimilar from, that of any state whose capacity to transform its surrounding environment is limited. Second, EUFSP is relational because of the ways in which the Union and the member states handle the contextual challenges. More than any state, the EU most distinctively seeks, pursues and sustains alliances, partnerships and dialogues with multiple interlocutors at various levels (global, regional, local); more than any other international organisation, the EU has at its disposal a panoply of instruments to selectively address political, social and economic dimensions of conflicts; and differently from any state or international organisation, EUFSP can be equally carried out by supranational institutions and member states. In these terms, the relational nature of EUFSP results from the interaction between the contextual factors and the EU's unique governance structures. 'Relational power' thus describes simultaneously the EU's structural dependence on its context as well as its resilience to the contextual challenges.

Conclusion

In the theoretical perspectives that we have reviewed in this chapter, we have detected a tendency to concentrate on the EU's norms and institutional structure as well as its resources as the main lens through which EU foreign and security policy can best be understood. While we do not contest the invaluable insights offered by these theories into how integration works and EUFSP operates, we suggest that the actual conduct of the EU in crisis and conflict management eludes rigorous theoretical characterisations and demands an analysis that sees EU foreign and security policy evolving in relation to structural factors in international affairs and their interplay with the domestic politics of EU countries. In light of this, we support the proposition that a complementary, outside-in perspective should be added to the inside-out perspectives dominant in most EU studies.[49]

The outside-in perspective is in line with recent trends in the literature as well as with pragmatist understandings of EUFSP, which increasingly acknowledge the "relational ontology of entanglement in the global register", the "advent of a multiplex world order", or a world in a constant state of "becoming", highlighting how such levels of complexity and dynamism blur outside/inside distinctions.[50] In continuity with these trends in International Relations and peace studies, we assume that EUFSP in crises and conflicts ultimately boils down to a deep interaction of EU institutions and member states with factors exogenous to the EU's institutional set-up. Such factors comprise an increasingly antagonistic multipolarity as well as fragmented regional politics, especially in areas surrounding the EU. These systemic factors interact directly with EU member states' domestic politics, contributing to processes of politicisation and, more broadly, to the reformulation (or re-affirmation) of domestic preferences.

Taken together, multipolar competition, regional fragmentation and internal contestation make up the context in which EU and national policymakers deal with crises and conflicts. Our assumption is that by examining how member states and institutions are constrained while trying to navigate, mitigate or resolve problems of policy arising from the contextual factors (individually or in combination with one another), we can complement the existing literature and contribute original insights into the nature of EUFSP. Complex global affairs – which brim with interdependence, entanglement, movement and change, and generate unpredictable pressures and cascading effects – require an understanding of the EU as a relational power, that is, an entity whose international actorness is inherently moulded by its interaction with, as well as adaptability and resilience to, external pressures.

In the next two chapters, we flesh out more concretely the two dimensions constituting the concept of relational power Europe: in Chapter 3, we focus on the EUFSP constitutive dependence on contextual challenges, while in Chapter 4 we move to EUFSP's equally constitutive resilience to them.

Notes

1 Andrew Moravcsik, "Preferences and Power in the European Community: A Liberal Intergovernmentalist Approach", *Journal of Common Market Studies,* Vol. 31, No. 4, December 1993, pp. 473–524 at p. 474, https://doi.org/10.1111/j.1468-5965.1993.tb00477.x.

2 Uwe Puetter, *The European Council and the Council. New Intergovernmentalism and Institutional Change*, Oxford, Oxford University Press, 2014. See also Sergio Fabbrini, "Catalysts of Integration – The Role of Core Intergovernmental Forums in EU Politics", *Journal of European Integration,* Vol. 38, No. 5, 2016, pp. 633–642, https://doi.org/10.1080/07036337.2016.1179294.

3 Christopher J. Bickerton, Dermot Hodson and Uwe Puetter, "The New Intergovernmentalism: European Integration in the Post-Maastricht Era", *Journal of Common Market Studies,* Vol. 53, No. 4, July 2014, pp. 703–722, https://doi.org/10.1111/jcms.12212. See also, Andrew Moravcsik, "Preferences, Power and Institutions in 21st-Century Europe", *Journal of Common Market Studies*, Vol. 56, No. 7, 2018, pp. 1648–1674, https://doi.org/10.1111/jcms.12804.

4 Adrian Hyde-Price, *Germany and European Order. Enlarging NATO and the EU*, Manchester/New York, Manchester University Press, 2000.
5 Anders Wivel and Ole Wæver, "The Power of Peaceful Change: The Crisis of the European Union and the Rebalancing of Europe's Regional Order", *International Studies Review*, Vol. 20, No. 2, June 2018, pp. 317–325, https://doi.org/10.1093/isr/viy027.
6 Mareike Kleine and Mark Pollack, "Liberal Intergovernmentalism and Its Critics", *Journal of Common Market Studies*, Vol. 56, No. 7, November 2018, pp. 1493–1509, https://doi.org/10.1111/jcms.12803.
7 Arne Niemann, *Explaining Decisions in the European Union*, Cambridge, Cambridge University Press, 2006.
8 Arne Niemann, "Neofunctionalism", in Marianne Riddervold, Jarle Trondal and Akasemi Newsome (eds), *The Palgrave Handbook of EU Crises*, Cham, Palgrave Macmillan, 2021, pp. 115–133 at p. 124 and ff.
9 Pol Morillas, "Autonomy in Intergovernmentalism: The Role of de Novo Bodies in External Action during the Making of the EU Global Strategy", *Journal of European Integration*, Vol. 42, No. 2, 2020, pp. 231–246, https://doi.org/10.1080/07036337.2019.1666116.
10 Monika Sus, "Supranational Entrepreneurs: The High Representative and the EU Global Strategy", *International Affairs,* Vol. 97, No. 3, May 2021, pp. 823–840, https://doi.org/10.1093/ia/iiab037.
11 Liesbeth Hooghe and Gary Marks, "Grand Theories of European Integration in the Twenty-First Century", *Journal of European Public Policy*, Vol. 26, No. 8, 2019, pp. 1113–1133, https://doi.org/10.1080/13501763.2019.1569711.
12 Mats Braun, "Postfunctionalism, Identity and the Visegrad Group", *Journal of Common Market Studies*, Vol. 58, No. 4, July 2020, pp. 925–940, https://doi.org/10.1111/jcms.12994. See also, Frank Schimmelfennig, "European Integration (Theory) in Times of Crisis. A Comparison of the Euro and Schengen Crises", *Journal of European Public Policy*, Vol. 25, No. 7, 2018, pp. 969–989, https://doi.org/10.1080/13501763.2017.1421252.
13 Ana E. Juncos and Karolina Pomorska, "Contesting Procedural Norms: The Impact of Politicisation on European Foreign Policy Cooperation", *European Security*, Vol. 30, No. 3, 2021, pp. 367–384, https://doi.org/10.1080/09662839.2021.1947799.
14 Montserrat Guibernau, "The Birth of a United Europe: On Why the EU Has Generated a 'Non-Emotional' Identity", *Nations and Nationalism*, Vol. 17, No. 2, 2011, pp. 302–315, https://doi.org/10.1111/j.1469-8129.2010.00477.x.
15 Theresa Kuhn, "Grand Theories of European Integration Revisited: Does Identity Politics Shape the Course of European Integration?", *Journal of European Public Policy*, Vol. 26, No. 8, 2019, pp. 1213–1230, https://doi.org/10.1080/13501763.2019.1622588.
16 Thomas Risse, "Social Constructivism and European Integration", in Antje Wiener and Thomas Diez (eds), *European Integration Theory*, 2nd ed., New York, Oxford University Press, 2009, pp. 144–160.
17 Heidi Maurer, Richard G. Whitman and Nicholas Wright, "The EU and the Invasion of Ukraine: A Collective Responsibility to Act?", *International* Affairs, Vol. 99, No. 1, 2023, pp. 219–238, https://doi.org/10.1093/ia/iiac262.

18 See, further, Mathieu Segers and Steven Van Hecke, *The Cambridge History of the European Union: Volume 2, European Integration Inside-Out,* Cambridge, Cambridge University Press, 2023.
19 For example, see Michael E. Smith, *Europe's Foreign and Security Policy: The Institutionalization of Cooperation*, Cambridge, Cambridge University Press, 2003.
20 Douglas Webber, "Trends in European Political (Dis)Integration. An Analysis of Postfunctionalist and Other Explanations", *Journal of European Public Policy*, Vol. 26, No. 8, 2019, pp. 1134–1152, https://doi.org/10.1080/13501763.2019.1576760.
21 François Duchêne, "The European Community and the Uncertainties of Interdependence", in Max Kohnstamm and Wolfgang Hager (eds), *A Nation Writ-Large? Foreign-Policy Problems before the European Community*, London/Basingstoke, Macmillan, 1973, pp. 1–21 at p. 19. See also, Francois Duchêne, "Europe's Role in World Peace", in Richard Mayne (ed.), *Europe Tomorrow. Sixteen Europeans Look Ahead*, London, Fontana, 1972, pp. 32–47.
22 Andrew Moravcsik, "Europe: The Quiet Superpower", in *French Politics*, Vol. 7, No. 3–4, September-December 2009, pp. 403–422, https://doi.org/10.1057/fp.2009.29.
23 Anu Bradford, *The Brussels Effect.* How the European Union Rules the World, Oxford/New York, Oxford University Press, 2020. See also, Chad Damro, "Market Power Europe", *Journal of European Public Policy*, Vol. 19, No. 5, 2012, pp. 682–699, https://doi.org/10.1080/13501763.2011.646779.
24 Hedley Bull, "Civilian Power Europe: A Contradiction in Terms?", *Journal of Common Market Studies*, Vol. 21, No. 2, December 1982, pp. 149–170 at p. 151, https://doi.org/10.1111/j.1468-5965.1982.tb00866.x.
25 Hedley Bull, "Civilian Power Europe: A Contradiction in Terms?", *Journal of Common Market Studies*, Vol. 21, No. 2, December 1982, pp. 149–170 at p. 151, https://doi.org/10.1111/j.1468-5965.1982.tb00866.x. See, further, Stelios Stavridis, "'Militarising' the EU: The Concept of Civilian Power Europe Revisited", *The International Spectator*, Vol. 36, No. 4, December 2001, pp. 43–50, https://doi.org/10.1080/03932720108456945.
26 Adrian Hyde-Price, "'Normative' Power Europe: A Realist Critique", *Journal of European Public Policy*, Vol. 13, No. 2, 2006, pp. 217–234 at p. 225, https://doi.org/10.1080/13501760500451634.
27 Douglas Barrie et al., "Europe's Defence Requires Offence", *Survival*, Vol. 63, No. 1, 2021, pp. 19–24, https://doi.org/10.1080/00396338.2021.1881249. See also, Helene Sjursen, "What Kind of Power?", *Journal of European Public Policy*, Vol. 13, No. 2, 2006, pp. 169–181, https://doi.org/10.1080/13501760500451584.
28 Asle Toje, "The European Union as a Small Power, or Conceptualizing Europe's Strategic Actorness", *Journal of European Integration*, Vol. 30, No. 2, 2008, pp. 199–215, https://doi.org/10.1080/07036330802005425. See also, Luis Simón, "Europe, the Rise of Asia and the Future of the Transatlantic Relationship", *International Security*, Vol. 91, No. 5, September 2015, pp. 969–989, https://doi.org/10.1111/1468-2346.12393.

29 Ian Manners, "Normative Power Europe: A Contradiction in Terms?", *Journal of Common Market Studies*, Vol. 40, No. 2, June 2002, pp. 235–258 at p. 253, https://doi.org/10.1111/1468-5965.00353.
30 Adrian Hyde-Price, "'Normative' Power Europe: A Realist Critique", *Journal of European Public Policy*, Vol. 13, No. 2, 2006, pp. 217–234 at p. 225, https://doi.org/10.1080/13501760500451634.
31 Richard G. Whitman (ed.), *Normative Power Europe. Empirical and Theoretical Perspectives*, Basingstoke, Palgrave Macmillan, 2011.
32 Raffaella A. Del Sarto, "Normative Empire Europe: The European Union, Its Borderlands, and the 'Arab Spring'", *Journal of Common Market Studies*, Vol. 54, No. 2, March 2016, pp. 215–232, https://doi.org/10.1111/jcms.12282; Marek Newman (ed.), *Democracy Promotion and the Normative Power Europe Framework. The European Union in South Eastern Europe, Eastern Europe, and Central Asia*, Cham, Springer, 2019.
33 Roberta Guerrina and Katharine A.M. Wright, "Gendering Normative Power Europe: Lessons of the Women, Peace and Security Agenda", *International Affairs*, Vol. 92, No. 2, 2016, pp. 293–312, https://doi.org/10.1111/1468-2346.12555.
34 Nathalie Tocci, *A Green and Global Europe*, Cambridge, Polity Press, 2022.
35 Granted, structural realism does point to the systemic pressures that determine state behaviour. But its account of structure is deterministic; in an anarchic international system with self-help dynamics, according to the realists, the EU is a mere instrument in the hands of the most powerful member states.
36 Sandra Lavenex and Marija-Liisa Öberg, "Third Country Influence on EU Law and Policymaking: Setting the Scene", *JCMS: Journal of Common Market Studies*, Vol. 61, No. 6, 2023, p. 1436.
37 They admit that the specific framework they develop would not be suited for accounting for the impact on EU policymaking of geopolitical factors (Lavenex and Öberg 2023, p. 1438).
38 This is a way to connect European Studies with non-Western centric sensitivities in International Relations, for example: Amitav Acharya, *Constructing Global Order Agency and Change in World Politics*, Cambridge University Press, 2018.
39 Steve Wood, "Pragmatic Power EUrope?", *Cooperation and Conflict*, Vol. 46, No. 2, 2011, pp. 242–261, https://doi.org/10.1177/0010836711406420
40 Ana E. Juncos, "Resilience as the New EU Foreign Policy Paradigm: A Pragmatist Turn?", *European Security*, Vol. 26, No. 1, 2017, pp. 1–18, https://doi.org/10.1080/09662839.2016.1247809.
41 Lucia A. Seybert and Peter J. Katzenstein, "Protean Power and Control Power: Conceptual Analysis", in Peter J. Katzenstein and Lucia A. Seybert (eds), *Protean Power. Exploring the Uncertain and Unexpected in World Politics*, Cambridge, Cambridge University Press, 2018, pp. 3–26.
42 Ana E. Juncos and Simon Frankel Pratt, "Pragmatist Power Europe: Resilience and Evolution in Planetary Organic Crisis", *Cooperation and Conflict*, 22 April 2024, https://doi.org/10.1177/00108367241244958.

43 Brigid Laffan, "Collective Power Europe? (The Government and Opposition/Leonard Schapiro Lecture 2022)", *Government and Opposition*, Vol. 58, No. 4, October 2023, pp. 623–640, https://doi.org/10.1017/gov.2022.52.

44 See also Claudia Wiesner, "Relations, Networks, and Entanglements: The Anthropocene as a Challenge to Modern Democratic Governance in Europe", in Corinne M. Flick (ed.), *Is the Open Society Sustainable in Case of Emergency?*, Munich, Convoco! Editions, 2024.

45 Pragmatist approaches have also been crucial to rethink peace-support operations as involving long-term and non-linear processes, where networks of actors cooperate and clash across both time and space: see Anna Jarstad, Johanna Söderström and Malin Åkebo, *Relational Peace Practices*, Manchester, Manchester University Press, 2023. See also, Pol Bargués, "Peacebuilding without Peace? On How Pragmatism Complicates the Practice of International Intervention", *Review of International Studies*, Vol. 46, No. 2, 2021, pp. 237–255, https://doi.org/10.1017/S0260210520000042; Ignasi Torrent, *Entangled Peace. UN Peacebuilding and the Limits of a Relational World*, Lanham, Rowman & Littlefield, 2021.

46 See, for instance, Susan Strange, *The Retreat of the State: The Diffusion of Power in the World Economy*, New York, Continuum, 1996.

47 Maria Gwynn, "Structural Power and International Regimes", *Journal of Political Power*, Vol. 12, No. 2, 2019, pp. 200–223.

48 Milja Kurki, "Relational Revolution and Relationality in IR: New Conversations", *Review of International Studies*, Vol. 48, No. 5, 2022, p. 824.

49 Richard Youngs, *The European Union and Global Politics*, London, Red Globe Press, 2021, pp. 192–193.

50 Amitav Acharya, "After Liberal Hegemony: The Advent of a Multiplex World Order", *Ethics & International Affairs*, Vol. 31, No. 3, 2017, pp. 271–285, https://doi.org/10.1017/S089267941700020X. See also, Debbie Lisle, "A Speculative Lexicon of Entanglement", *Millennium*, Vol. 49, No. 3, 2021, pp. 435–461 at p. 443, https://doi.org/10.1177/03058298211021919; Jason Ralph, *On Global Learning. Pragmatic Constructivism, International Practice and the Challenge of Global Governance*, Cambridge, Cambridge University Press, 2023.

3 An outside-in perspective of EU foreign and security policy

An overwhelming empirical fact stands out when considering Europe's predicament in the 21st century and especially since the 2010s: the staggering growth in number and intensity of the crises and conflicts impinging on European security interests, directly and indirectly. Indeed, so prominent has crisis and conflict management become that it can now be regarded as a major component of EU foreign and security policy.

In this chapter, we start off with the observation that the EU and its member states have struggled to develop and sustain effective crisis and management policies. We argue that underlying the EU's difficulties are the three contextual factors of multipolar competition, regional fragmentation and internal contestation. Certainly, other factors such as economic interdependence, cultural diversity or ideological rivalry also shape the international environment and consequently the context of EU foreign and security policy.[1] Yet the concepts of multipolar competition, regional fragmentation and internal contestation can be accommodated with economic interdependence or ideological rivalry, which they can merge with, supplement or subsume depending on the circumstances. For example, in the EU's dealings with Russia and the United States' engagements with China, economic interdependence did not serve as a deterrent to conflict; rather, it was weaponised (as seen in Ukraine) or it failed to mitigate increasing hostility (regarding Taiwan and the South China Sea). Conversely, ideological and cultural disparities are integral to, and influenced by, interstate competition and regional fragmentation. For instance, Russia's aggression of Ukraine not only shifted the European power balance but also transformed the EU-Russia dynamic from one of cooperation to one of systemic competition. Similarly, the resurgence of major power rivalries not only

DOI: 10.4324/9781003559467-4

challenged unipolarity but also undermined the West's construction of a rules-based and liberal world order.[2]

While not exhaustive, multipolar competition, regional fragmentation and internal contestation offer a broad framework for understanding the forces that undermine the cohesion and effectiveness of EUFSP in crises and conflicts. In the next three sections, we dwell on each of the contextual factors and highlight the ways in which they worked as constraints on the EU's crisis and conflict management capacity, thereby highlighting the first dimension of the relational nature of EUFSP: the contextual factors perform a fundamental function in the constitution of the EU's actorness in international security. The relational nature of EUFSP here is to be understood as expressing its constitutive dependence on the context in which it unfolds.

The pressure of multipolar competition

Multipolarity is the process by which power – economic, military and technological – is distributed across several countries.[3] The concept is usually understood as having a global scope, but, in fact, it is often a more accurate depiction of regional realities.[4] It is in regions after all that the distribution of power across multiple centres is the most visible.[5] Some countries may have no capacity of global power projection, yet their material resources can still be sufficient to shape events in their own neighbourhood; besides, influence is also transmitted regionally through non-material assets such as cultural proximities, religious or ethnic commonalities and societal links at large.

By virtue of sheer arithmetic, multipolarity complicates the exercise of multilateral governance. When many power centres are involved in the process, consensus and shared interests are harder to find. Yet there is no automatism between multipolarity and the erosion of multilateral governance. The latter happens only when multipolarity imparts a competitive turn to interstate relations. Multipolar competition is driven by conflicting views of order, global and regional alike.[6] Crises and conflicts consequently are no longer construed as transnational problems for which the international community at large bears responsibility, but arenas of strategic confrontation. In fact, conflicts and crises are not just augmented by multipolar competition but may also directly originate from it. This is especially the case when competition encompasses the whole relationship between the rival powers and is dominated by a zero-sum logic, whereby conflict or crisis resolution is invariably framed in terms of wins or losses of the parties with a stake in the issue at hand.[7]

Multipolar competition affects the crisis/conflict management capacity of the EU and its member states in several respects. The first and most obvious one is that it magnifies the weakness of the EU's modest military capacity: even factoring in the resources of the militarily largest member states such as France, the Union lacks an important – arguably critical – asset to sustain competition with rivals.[8] The crises and conflicts in which the EU has been involved in the past decade offer ample empirical evidence of all this.

In the South China Sea, where the United States and China are at odds over the latter's aggressive approach to sustain its claims to disputed islands, European naval military capabilities had little to offer. This implied that the EU's role in crisis management in the area was marginal.[9] This trajectory was obviously more pronounced in instances in which geopolitical competition took on a direct military dimension – from Libya to Syria to, more recently, tensions in the Gulf of Oman and the Red Sea. But even in the Russia-Ukraine war, in which European mobilisation of hard power assets has actually been remarkable, multipolar competition has laid bare the limits of EU's military capacity.[10]

By summer 2024, two and half years after the start of the invasion, EU institutions and individual member states had delivered over 40 billion euros' worth of military assistance to Kyiv.[11] While impressive, European arms and ammunition transfers only made a difference because they were complemented with the larger and more sophisticated aid provided by the United States. Had the latter dried out, the EU would have been in no position to sustain the intense competition with Russia over Ukraine in which it had engaged since the start of the war. The possible scenarios that project that US support for Ukraine might dwindle reveal European military weakness. The United States could feel compelled to move its resources to Asia, should the risk of a conflagration with China there grow. Perversely, the EU member states' limited ability to invest and spend more and better in defence capabilities may actually fuel US disengagement, as insinuated by a growing section of the Republican Party.[12]

A second consequence of the heightening of multipolar competition is the erosion of multilateral and constructive resolution of controversies.[13] Struggling to connect its own efforts with broader inclusive frameworks, the EU and its member states were often compelled to rely on narrower platforms, which tend to have a scarcer legitimacy in the eyes of conflict parties and often a reduced capacity to influence events on the ground.

Take the case of the Joint Comprehensive Plan of Action (JCPOA), the United Nations Security Council-endorsed deal that in 2015 put severe (though temporary) limits to Iran's ability to divert its nuclear programme to military uses. A triumph of multilateral diplomacy, to which the Europeans had contributed significantly (as explained in the next chapter),[14] this multilateral deal eventually faltered under the strain of extreme geopolitical and ideological rivalries.[15] First came the United States' decision, spurred by Iran's rivals (especially Israel), to ignore its multilateral commitments and quit the deal in 2018; then transatlantic tensions made it impossible for the Europeans to maintain legitimate EU-Iran trade; finally, the West-Russia clash over Ukraine undermined what was left of multilateral efforts at restoring the deal.[16] With the JCPOA in tatters, the EU's contribution to the management of the Iranian nuclear dossier as well as other issues of concern involving the Islamic Republic, including its ballistic arsenal and regional policies, shrank dramatically.[17]

Multipolar tensions weakened EU-championed multilateral crisis and conflict management in other instances too. The initial consensus in the UN Security Council, which authorised NATO's intervention in Libya in 2011, was short-lived, and multipolar tensions (which extended to regional players, most notably Egypt and Turkey) consistently undermined the formulas for conflict resolution that the UN managed to concoct in the years thereafter.[18] No inclusive framework was ever created over Syria, mostly due to Western and Arab ostracism towards Iran, competition with Russia and profound divergences with Turkey over the role of Syria's Kurdish fighters.[19]

The cases above also point to a third key weakness exposed by multipolar competition. In a world of competing poles, crisis and conflict parties look elsewhere for alternative options to those presented by the EU and its member states through incentives, opportunities or coercive measures.

For Iran, the prospect of normalised economic relations and political dialogue with Europe was arguably the greatest incentive to enter the nuclear deal. But the EU's leverage on Iran depended on its ability to deliver economic benefits and the absence of strong political and economic alternatives for Tehran. Both conditions vanished in the vortex of greater multipolar competition triggered by the United States' decision to quit the JCPOA in 2018. US extraterritorial sanctions forced EU banks and companies to fall in line with a trade embargo on Iran, curtailing the EU's ability to provide positive incentives.[20] In parallel, China and Russia gradually subordinated their non-proliferation concerns to the imperative of confronting the United States, whereby they resolved to give Iran political and economic depth to absorb Western pressure.[21] After Russia invaded Ukraine, Iran provided Russia with military assistance (especially drones and drone manufacture know-how), which widened the gap with the Europeans. These interconnected processes of geopolitical rivalry contributed to insulating Iran from European pressure, while making strategically unviable for the EU to offer incentives as it had prior to the signing of the JCPOA, when multipolar rivalry was less acute.[22]

Shifting configurations of multipolar competition diminished European influence in many other cases. In Syria,* a battleground for larger geopolitical contests, the Assad regime was able to shrug off European sanctions and diplomatic isolation thanks to the support of Iran and Russia.[23] Likewise, European states had no influence over the Islamist opposition to Assad based in Idlib because Turkey has turned that city and its surrounding area into a buffer against both Assad and Syria's Kurds.[24] In Libya, fierce multipolar rivalries between the government in Tripoli, supported by Turkey and Qatar, and its rival based in Tobruk, supported by Egypt, Russia and the United Arab Emirates, played into deep intra-European divisions (notably between France and Italy) to shrink EU influence over conflict parties.[25] In Ethiopia, the federal government could flatly reject EU calls for de-escalation during the 2020–2022 war against Tigray's rebels thanks to military support from Turkey, the United Arab Emirates and Iran. Meanwhile Russia and China's diplomatic cover in the UN Security Council allowed the Ethiopian government to resist European-championed pressure to let humanitarian aid into rebel-held zones.[26] A similar power game, but on a larger scale, played out in Venezuela. Russia and China went the extra-mile to help the embattled regime of Nicolás Maduro to evade sanctions and deflect Western demands for national reconciliation talks with opposition forces.[27]

In sum, multipolar competition complicates EU crisis and conflict management. It magnifies the EU and its member states' weakest aspects, such as their perennially incipient military capabilities. It also undermines those aspects in which the EU is relatively strong, making coalitions and collective responses difficult to initiate and sustain.

* this book was completed before the fall of Assad in December 2024

Multipolar competition also frustrates the EU's capacity for crisis and conflict management in more indirect ways. As a major disaggregation factor in regions and even individual states, multipolar competition contributes to the proliferation of transnational challenges that erode state authority and regional governance. It thus intersects with the dynamics of regional fragmentation that have emerged and consolidated in recent years and which further contribute to constraining European foreign and security policy.

The pressure of regional fragmentation

Just like multipolarity and multipolar competition, the phenomenon of fragmentation has received considerable scholarly attention in the last years.[28] It describes the process by which the state is no longer capable of setting and enforcing laws.[29] The state fractures across multiple power centres, ranging from alternative institutions claiming to be the only locus of state legitimacy to separatist entities or rival local authorities pushing for more autonomy.[30] Nonstate actors, such as armed militias (at times an extension of political parties), criminal networks or terrorist organisations, may also exercise authority in certain areas.[31] Regional fragmentation occurs insofar as the erosion or collapse of state authority in one country 'infects', like a contagion, neighbouring states. Instability then spans across borders. Underlying this process may be a low level of political, social and economic integration, the inability of the regional hegemon to bring about order or a wobbly regional balance of power.[32] Indeed, as anticipated above, state fragmentation combines with interstate rivalries – often along a circular pattern of causality – to hollow out governance mechanisms or prevent them from being established in the first place.

Conflict management, always an excruciatingly difficult task, is doubly complicated in fragmented regions.[33] Prolonged conflicts in areas where state control is weak and inefficient engender severe humanitarian consequences such as depressing or even collapsing local economies, augmenting the aid requirements of local populations, spawning massive migration flows, stimulating illicit trafficking or providing fertile ground for radicalisation.[34] With multiple actors involved, both state and nonstate, spoilers abound; even when institutions are reestablished, they may suffer from dubious legitimacy. All this bears heavily on the EU's conflict and crisis management capacity.[35] Rarely, if ever, do EU institutions and member states manage to integrate their responses to conflicts so as to address holistically the multifaceted challenges emanating from fragmentation.[36]

A major problem in this regard is the proliferation of interlocutors at all levels (state, subnational and regional) with diverging and even opposed agendas. This compels the EU and the member states to take decisions about whom to engage that may undermine the overall legitimacy and consistency of their approaches. The legitimacy issue cuts both ways: engagement with specific state or nonstate actors may be unacceptable for the EU and its member states (or for just some of them) or, alternatively, it may be perceived by other conflict actors as delegitimising EU peacebuilding efforts. This constraint can be easily tracked in the efforts that EU and member states put into managing a number of crises and conflicts.[37]

In Syria, the issue manifested itself in various forms. From the very beginning, EU countries agreed upon a policy of no-contact with the Assad regime. Initially, this made sense as the EU aligned with the United States and Syria's Arab rivals in lending support to a broad coalition of opposition forces. However, direct interaction with local actors was always limited and eventually faded away as it became increasingly hard to find a common agenda – besides Assad's removal – with an opposition undergoing internal fracturing and Islamist radicalisation. EU states kept their policy of no-contact in place even as they shifted their priorities to migration and the fight against the Islamic State in Iraq and al-Sham (ISIS), and Syria became ever more the epicentre of multipolar competition.[38] The unwillingness to engage with Assad was an important reason for which the Europeans never seriously contemplated the possibility of establishing any kind of interaction with the Astana framework, a format set by Russia, Iran and Turkey, in spite of the latter's potential to bring down violence in Syria. The incompatibility of the EU's approach with the Astana format redirected EUFSP towards Syria from conflict management to support for the US-championed policy of preventing the Assad regime from gaining control of the Kurdish-held north-eastern part of the country.[39] In other words, EUFSP towards Syria eventually turned into a factor contributing to Syria's internal fragmentation.

In Libya, Europeans were compelled to reassess their engagement strategies with local actors several times. The Transitional National Council established in opposition to long-standing autocratic leader Muhammar Gaddafi, which EU countries (especially France) enthusiastically supported in the early phase of the civil conflict, proved incapable of enabling a peaceful transition into a pluralist and open government. The problem of 'interlocutor selection' exploded after the contested 2014 elections resulted in the formation of rival governments in Tripoli and Tobruk. Nothing illustrates more vividly how this issue harmed EU conflict management efforts than the fact that Italy and France supported opposing warring factions for years. After German mediation, eventually the EU found an agreement on an inclusive engagement strategy, yet the damage of diminished EU leverage in Libya could not be re-absorbed completely as in the meantime Libya's different groups had found other patrons, most notably Turkey and Russia (as recalled above).[40]

The dilemma of selecting the 'right' interlocutors out of competing agendas for the European approach to conflict management also emerged in Venezuela. Here, the initial position of most EU member states was to deny legitimacy to the Maduro regime and recognising an alternative president. Even if coordinated with the United States and a coalition of Latin American countries, this strategy did not yield results in terms of restoring democratic practices in Venezuela. Instead of pluralising and becoming more amenable to a process of national reconciliation, the regime actually became more intransigent. Subsequently, the EU altered its course, endorsing a Norway-led negotiation process and engaging with the Venezuelan government in order to deploy an election monitoring mission. This shift was possible due to a lower level of fragmentation. Regional divisions, which had hindered multilateral efforts of Latin American organisations to restore some political and economic stability to Venezuela, eased after Brazil and Colombia elected leaders who scaled down the confrontation with the Maduro regime.[41]

A second, more common constraint emanating from fragmentation revolves around the tension between conflict management tasks and the handling of other issues of concern that are related to, but also separable from, the conflict at hand. Fragmentation creates a multiplicity of challenges across a wide array of policy fields, ranging from a surge in migration flows to the expansion of criminal activities or the establishment of safe havens for terrorist groups. EU member state governments are thus often confronted with trade-offs that invariably lead them to accord preference to one issue over another, while diminishing their commitment to conflict resolution.

Libya and Syria are excellent vantage points from which this constraint can be appreciated. Diverging priorities lay at the heart of the French-Italian divide over Libya, which severely undermined consistency and impact of EUFSP there.[42] Italy leaned towards the internationally recognised government in Tripoli also because the latter controlled the coasts from which migrants departed for Italian ports, as well as because most of Italian energy assets were located in Western Libya.[43] Instead, France was willing to lend support to Khalifa Haftar, the Cyrenaica-based strongman, mostly because it saw him as a safer bet in the fight against Islamist extremism, its main security concern after the November 2015 terrorist attacks in Paris.[44]

EU member states displayed greater unity over the civil war in Syria, and yet crisis management was eventually relegated to a third-order priority. Conflict resolution efforts – which had been sustained in the early phase of the war – thinned out as most energies and resources were spent on stemming the flow of migrants leaving or transiting through Syria. Rather than directly addressing the conflict, the EU and member states put forward a region-based approach to halting migration to Europe, establishing deals with neighbouring countries – most notably with Turkey in 2016 – to address the humanitarian emergency situation alongside increasing border security to fend off the ISIS menace.[45]

A final problem concerns the production of shared knowledge of the conflict or crisis in order to tailor policies to local conditions. In Ethiopia, for instance, studies have shown how the EU failed to anticipate the outbreak of the civil war between the federal government and the Tigray People's Liberation Front (TPLF) because its sources of knowledge about Ethiopia's internal situation were both limited and biased.[46] The Europeans believed their own narrative of Prime Minister Abiy Ahmed as a liberal champion for inclusive peace (in light of the political reforms at home and the peace accord with Eritrea he had promoted) rather than seeing him as a coalition leader playing hardball in Ethiopia's highly fragmented and polarised ethnic and political landscape. The European initial understanding of the war was informed by a widespread perception that Abiy had betrayed their trust. It also mattered that the EU had developed ties with the TPLF during the latter's decades-old spell in power before Abiy's rise in 2018, which led senior EU officials to lean towards pro-Tigray views. This led the EU to initially put the blame for the outbreak of violence squarely on the federal government, which created a gap in trust that the EU was unable to repair, even after making a course correction later on.[47]

The problem of generating common knowledge about local contexts can hardly be attributed to negligence only, or even mainly. Even considering the diplomatic assets of member states, European resources to gather intelligence are limited, information-sharing is slow and diplomatic personnel deployed on the grounds rotates on a regular basis, whereby the acquired knowledge may, at least partially, get lost during the turnover cycles.[48] Furthermore, conflict areas characterised by high levels of fragmentation tend to be not just overly complex but constantly evolving, and this makes contextual knowledge an ever-moving target. In Libya, for instance, EU member states confronted the challenge (amongst others) of developing a comprehensive understanding of power dynamics amongst a multitude of armed militias organised along tribal lines.[49] In Syria's civil war, where alliances between the warring parties were more stable, EU countries failed to predict the Islamist radicalisation of many of the groups into which the anti-Assad opposition splintered.[50]

The constraints imposed on EUFSP by fragmentation are significant, especially as they inevitably interplay with other contextual factors. While usually associated with risks resulting from multipolar competition, state and regional fragmentation also intertwines with the domestic politics of EU member states. This is the third contextual factor, intra-EU contestation, which further dents the crisis and conflict management capacity of the Union.

The pressure of internal contestation

Scholars have long established that the permissive consensus in which European integration unfolded for decades has faded, giving way to a more divided and at times polarised public debate.[51] "Constraining dissensus" has come to demarcate the potential for EU action in a number of policy domains, and foreign and security policy has been no exception.[52]

Internal contestation mostly arises from the difficulty of reconciling domestically construed interests with interests that derive from EU membership. But it can also be instrumental in nature. Nationalist or populist parties, in particular, out of ideological conviction or for reasons of electoral expediency, are inclined to politicise dissent. Sometimes they contest not just individual policies but shared and established norms and practices of the EU, if not the Union itself.[53] When put to the test, this seemingly extreme form of contestation often reveals itself to be more performative than substantial, and therefore not insurmountable.[54] Still, at times it actually is insurmountable and contributes to undermining the collective commitment to developing policies of common interest.[55]

Internal contestation affects EU crisis management efforts at various stages: problem framing, agenda setting, policy formulation and policy implementation.[56] Member state governments can construe foreign policy issues in ways that resonate with domestic audiences but are incompatible with the prevalent views inside the EU; they can prevent the EU from acting on specific issues or limit EU policy to peripheral aspects; and they may pay lip-service to a policy line agreed upon at the EU level but comply with it selectively or not at all.

Once again, the constraints put by internal contestation on EU foreign and security policy can be observed when examining the practice of crisis and conflict management.[57] The deterioration of the international security environment, exemplified by the fragmentation of regions across the EU's borders and exacerbated by multipolar rivalries, has given member states continuous occasions to quarrel. Contestation in these instances arises when member states have powerful domestic incentives to limit participation in EU crisis and conflict management efforts or not to invest in them altogether.[58] The domestic incentives to question European policies may reflect a national broad consensus, which is incompatible with the position of the other members. Alternatively, they may stem from internal divisions of regional or political nature or between public opinion and elites.[59] We have singled out three main sources of domestically-induced contestation of EUFSP.

The first stems from the perception that external conflicts have some similarity with domestic ones, as may be the case with conflicts between central authorities and independentist movements. Member state governments are extremely reluctant to support EU policies that, while making sense in the context of managing specific crises or conflicts, would have negative repercussions for the management of their own internal political divides. While rare, contestation arising from this source tends to be extremely rigid.[60] The case in point is the Kosovo-Serbia dispute. EU conflict resolution was seriously affected by the outright refusal of five member states to recognise Kosovo's independence for fear of setting a precedent for internal separatist movements (in the Basque country and Catalonia for Spain, Hungarian areas for Romania and Slovakia, Northern Cyprus for Cyprus and, in solidarity with the latter, Greece).[61] Non-recognition prevented the EU from making full use of its incentives (for instance, the Union was forced to narrow down the scope of the 2015 Stabilisation and Association Agreement with Kosovo only to matters of exclusive EU competences). Worse, these states indirectly gave cover to Serbia's position over Kosovo, complicating both Kosovo and Serbia's accession to the EU, a problem that became more acute due to the reduction of democratic standards in Serbia and its growing ties with Russia.[62]

Another, more common source of EUFSP contestation is party ideology. Governing coalitions in member states may find certain conflict management policies unacceptable ideologically or harmful to their political relations with one or more conflict parties.[63] An example in this regard is the refusal by a number of EU countries (initially nine, eventually just Cyprus and Italy) to recognise the leader of the opposition to the Maduro regime as Venezuela's legitimate president in 2019. The position of the contesters was not motivated by a divergence of goals – in fact, no EU countries accepted Maduro's reconfirmation as president through a presumably rigged election. Instead, it was an ideological opposition to a move that was perceived as a form of regime change engineered by the United States and its allies in Europe and Latin America. Contestation of the policy came from US-sceptic ruling parties, mostly left-wing or anti-establishment populist forces, as in the case of Italy's Five Star Movement.[64] The incident was by no means the main factor for the EU's modest influence over events in Venezuela; still, it dented its credibility in the eyes of both regime and opposition.[65]

Another example of politics-driven contestation, and one with much graver consequences, can be found when examining the engagement with the Israeli-Palestinian conflict. The EU's long-standing commitment to a two-state solution was inexorably hollowed out of meaning by the fierce resistance of a number of EU member states to single out and condemn – let alone punish – Israel's control over, and continuous settlement expansion in, Palestinian lands.[66] Divisions also emerged every time violence flared up in Gaza, including the Israel-Hamas war that began in October 2023, with the EU often failing to muster internal consensus for joint calls for ceasefires.[67]

While contestation came from different EU member states, the four Visegrád countries – Poland, Slovakia and especially the Czech Republic and Hungary – stood out. Not only did they block or water down common positions but also refused to comply with established EU policies (for instance, on labelling goods produced in Israeli settlements). Ideological affinities between ruling parties largely explain their support for Israel, especially as the latter veered ever more to right-wing nativism. Populist parties in the Visegrád countries (mostly right-wing) conflated their fierce opposition to migration from Muslim countries and concerns about Islamist-rooted terrorism with Israel's antagonism towards the Palestinians and fight against extremist groups like Hamas.[68] Political links were especially strong between the far-right government of Hungary's Viktor Orbán and Binyamin Netanyahu, Israel's dominant political figure since 2009, who gradually merged his conservative ideology with an illiberal agenda.[69]

Hungary's domestic politics was also the origin of contestation of EU policies towards the Ukraine war. Orbán's government resisted the adoption of EU sanctions against Russia, often seeking special exemptions before giving in. Hungary also opposed the provision of financial aid to Ukraine. This contestation had its roots in Orbán's embrace of Eurosceptic illiberal and ultranationalist conservatism (incidentally, also championed by Russian President Vladimir Putin) and his concern that a Russian defeat in Ukraine could eventually destabilise his own authoritarian grip on power.[70] To be sure, the impact of Hungary's contestation on EUFSP towards Ukraine was fairly limited.[71] It was not insignificant though. Hungary repeatedly delayed decisions, prohibited weapons transfers through its territory and contributed to spreading war narratives fiercely critical of Ukraine, the United States and the EU itself.

A third source of domestic-driven contestation of EUFSP lies in the relationship between elites and the public. Elites could be concerned that effective crisis resolution policies involve choices that significant sections of the public opinion would not support, and therefore block or delay them.[72]

An example was the pause on the enlargement process – the most effective tool for resolving the conflict between Kosovo and Serbia – imposed for a while by French President Emmanuel Macron. He was afraid that his political opponents would use scarce public support for EU enlargement against him.[73] Another example is Germany's shift in 2015–2016 from accepting large numbers of Syrian refugees to a strict border control policy, culminating in the 2016 migration control agreement with Turkey. The German government changed tack in the face of growing internal opposition and obstruction by other EU member states to an open-door policy.[74] The policy U-turn, entirely due to domestic politicisation (both within Germany and by other member states), actually averted an internal fracture within the EU. However, it also weakened the EU's management of the Syrian conflict by dispersing the international credit generated by Germany's initial welcoming stance and by giving Turkey greater leverage over the EU itself, as recalled above.[75]

Elite-public interactions that generate EUFSP contestation can also reflect a desire by elites to play along widespread and deeply rooted sentiments in large sections of the public opinion irrespective of party allegiances. Two instances of this kind of domestically induced contestation are observable again in Germany. The lingering strength of a pacifist and non-interventionist constituency, a legacy of Germany's role in starting World War II, was a main reason for the government's reluctance to transfer to Ukraine offensive weapons that could be used to target Russian territory.[76] Similarly, the elevation of Israel's security to *raison d'être* of the Federal Republic itself, a relatively recent process with its roots in the widely felt need to atone for the Holocaust, greatly complicated EU efforts to find a common voice on Palestine. This became clearly visible after Hamas' 7 October 2023 attack on Israel, which triggered an instinctive hardening of the German government position of unconditional defence of Israel even if its formal commitment to a Palestinian state was unchanged.[77] Germany's refusal to contemplate any pressure on Israel exacerbated the profound intra-EU divisions on how to react to the utter devastation that Israel unleashed on Gaza in retaliation.[78]

In sum, there are numerous instances in which internal contestation has constrained EUFSP for reasons that are not directly related to the specific crises or conflicts at hand. Member states may support the overall goal of conflict resolution but still hamper it for purely domestic reasons. In practice, however, internal contestation dynamics are hardly separable from the systemic factors of multipolar rivalry and regions' fragmentation. This interaction between factors is key to our concluding argument.

Conclusion

Geopolitical rivalry and fragmentation are certainly no novelties in international relations, and internal contestation of EU foreign and security policy has been a constant since the EU was created. However, from the late 2000s onwards all these factors grew in intensity and, more critically, so did their interplay. Indeed, it is possible to track mutually reinforcing dynamics between competition, fragmentation and contestation in most instances of conflicts that we have mentioned in this chapter, even if the relative weight of each and the intensity of the interplay obviously vary.

The nexus between multipolar competition and regional fragmentation is profound – in fact, it is so strong that the two factors fuel each other in a vicious circle of circular causality. The breakdown of state authority in some areas creates opportunities for global and regional powers to fill security vacuums. As arenas for multipolar competition proliferate, interstate rivalries deepen. This trend was evident in the Middle East, particularly in Syria, the territorial fragmentation of which eventually came to reflect an uneasy balance between rival 'poles': Russia and Iran supported Assad, Turkey the Islamist rebels based in Idlib, and the United States and a few European countries the Kurds. As we have seen, the multipolar contest playing out in that fragmented country compounded European weaknesses – modest military capabilities, reduced dependence on conflict parties and difficulties in the selection of interlocutors.

The fragmentation-competition dynamic operates in reverse as well, as global and regional powers actively back breakaway factions, rebels and armed groups in order to gain strategic advantages over their rivals. A main case in point is Libya. Here, European difficulties in managing a collapsing country in which external powers backed rival factions were further augmented by intra-EU contestation, so much so that the French-Italian divide eventually contributed to Libya's fragmentation. Notably, Libyan actors engaged themselves in shifting alliances, playing off external powers against each other, thus creating a vicious cycle between competition, fragmentation and contestation dynamics.[79]

There are other ways in which intra-EU contestation intermingled with fragmentation dynamics. The refusal by some member states to acknowledge unilateral declarations of independence (such as in the case of Kosovo) or to recognise opposition figures as legitimate leaders in other countries (as seen in Venezuela), while rooted in domestic politics, hindered the formation of a cohesive EU policy and initiatives for regional integration.

Intra-EU contestation is also linked to multipolar competition. Member state governments may have domestic motivations to challenge EU foreign and security policies to enhance their standing with non-EU nations. For example, many EU states refrained from retaliatory actions against the extraterritorial sanctions imposed by the United States on EU-Iran trade, fearing they would alienate their primary security ally, although that fatally undermined their efforts to keep Iran inside the nuclear deal. Moreover, internal disputes were rarely solely internal affairs, as external powers continuously interfered in the domestic politics of member states to derail, dilute or slow down EU foreign policymaking. Russia's relentless disinformation and election meddling, for instance, undoubtedly impacted the EU's conflict management efforts over the Donbas before the 2022 large-scale invasion. Even after that, it contributed to eroding domestic support for the defence of Ukraine, thereby constraining EU governments' options – or at least raising their political costs.

While the three factors describe different realities producing specific constraints on EUFSP, their co-existence, combination and interaction is what ultimately constitutes the context against which European policymakers take decisions and intervene in conflict-affected societies. Accordingly, we assume the efficiency and sustainability of EUFSP in conflict management to be a function of the ability of EU and national policymakers to utilise EUFSP governance structures and resources to contain, mitigate or overcome the constraints emanating from that volatile and challenging context. Rather than focusing on the competences or the capabilities of EU institutions and member states, our emphasis is on the process of dealing with constraints that are exogenous to the EU's institutional set-up. In the next chapter, we consider how the various strategies, tactics and practices to handle the contextual challenges articulate the EU as a 'relational power' and contribute to shaping its peculiar actorness in international security.

Notes

1 On economic interdependence, see (amongst others) Hugh White, *The China Choice. Why We Should Share Power*, Oxford, Oxford University Press, 2013. On cultural diversity, see (amongst others) Christopher Coker, *The Rise of the Civilizational State*, Cambridge/Medford, Polity Press, 2019. On ideological rivalry, see (amongst others) Arta Moeini, "America: The Last Ideological Empire", in *Compact Magazine*, 8 July 2022.

2 Nuno P. Monteiro, "World Order across the End of the Cold War", in Nuno P. Monteiro and Fritz Bartel (eds), *Before and After the Fall. World Politics and the End of the Cold War*, Cambridge, Cambridge University Press,

2021, pp. 338–360; Adrian Pabst, *Liberal World Order and Its Critics. Civilisational States and Cultural Commonwealths*, London/New York, Routledge, 2019.

3 Charles A. Kupchan, *No One's World. The West, the Rising Rest, and the Coming Global Turn*, Oxford/New York, Oxford University Press, 2012; Ian Bremmer, *Every Nation for Itself. Winners and Losers in a G-Zero World*, London, Portfolio/Penguin, 2012; Riccardo Alcaro, John Peterson and Ettore Greco (eds), *The West and the Global Power Shift. Transatlantic Relations and Global Governance*, Basingstoke/New York, Palgrave Macmillan, 2016; Oliver Stuenkel, *Post-Western World. How Emerging Powers Are Remaking Global Order*, Cambridge/Malden, Polity Press, 2016; Amitav Acharya, *The End of American World Order*, 2nd ed., Cambridge/Medford, Polity Press, 2018; Zachary Paikin, "Great Power Rivalry and the Weakening of Collective Hegemony: Revisiting the Relationship between International Society and International Order", *Cambridge Review of International Affairs*, Vol. 34, No. 1, 2021, pp. 22–45, https://doi.org/10.1080/09557571.2020.1720602.

4 Barry Buzan, "How Regions Were Made, and the Legacies for World Politics: An English School Reconnaissance", in Thazha V. Paul (ed.), *International Relations Theory and Regional Transformation*, Cambridge, Cambridge University Press 2012, pp. 22–46; Stephen G. Brooks and William C. Wohlforth, "The Myth of Multipolarity", *Foreign Affairs*, Vol. 102, No. 3, May/June 2023, pp. 76–91.

5 Simon Schunz, Sieglinde Gstöhl and Luk Van Langenhove, "Between Cooperation and Competition: Major Powers in Shared Neighbourhoods", *Contemporary Politics*, Vol. 24, No. 1, 2018, pp. 1–13, https://doi.org/10.1080/13569775.2017.1408174.

6 Graeme P. Herd (ed.), *Great Powers and Strategic Stability in the 21st Century. Competing Visions of World Order*, London/New York, Routledge, 2010; Riccardo Alcaro (ed.), *The Liberal Order and Its Contestations. Great Powers and Regions Transiting in a Multipolar Era*, London/New York, Routledge 2018; Alexander Lukin, *Russia and China. The New Rapprochement*, Cambridge, Polity Press, 2018.

7 Kristina Kausch, "Competitive Multipolarity in the Middle East", *The International Spectator*, Vol. 50, No. 3, 2015, pp. 1–15, https://doi.org/10.1080/03932729.2015.1055927. See also, Sten Rynning, "The False Promise of Continental Concert: Russia, the West and the Necessary Balance of Power", *International Affairs*, Vol. 91, No. 3, 2015, pp. 539–552; Richard Youngs, *Europe's Eastern Crisis. The Geopolitics of Asymmetry*, Cambridge, Cambridge University Press, 2017; Bilahari Kausikan, "The Arena", *Foreign Affairs,* Vol. 100, No. 2, March/April 2021, pp. 186–191.

8 Hugo Meijer and Stephen G. Brooks, "Illusions of Autonomy: Why Europe Cannot Provide for Its Security If the United States Pulls Back", *International Security*, Vol. 45, No. 4, yn 2021, pp. 7–43, https://doi.org/10.1162/isec_a_00405.

9 Zachary Paikin, "Multipolar Competition and the Rules-based Order: Probing the Limits of EU Foreign and Security Policy in the South China Sea",

The International Spectator, Vol. 59, No. 1, 2024, pp. 161–178, https://doi.org/10.1080/03932729.2023.2280598.

10 Paula Alvarez-Couceiro, "Europe at a Strategic Disadvantage: A Fragmented Defense Industry", in *War on the Rocks*, 18 April 2023, https://warontherocks.com/?p=28598. See also, Alessandro Marrone (ed.), *Russia-Ukraine War's Strategic Implications*, Rome, IAI, February 2024, https://www.iai.it/en/node/18118.

11 Kiel Institute for the World Economy, *Ukraine Support Tracker*, updated on 6 August 2024, https://www.ifw-kiel.de/topics/war-against-ukraine/ukraine-support-tracker.

12 Arancha González Laya et al., "*Trump-Proofing Europe*", in *Foreign Affairs*, 24 February 2024, https://www.foreignaffairs.com/node/1131310.

13 Zaki Laïdi, "Towards a Post-Hegemonic World: The Multipolar Threat to the Multilateral Order", *International Politics*, Vol. 51, No. 3, May 2014, pp. 350–365, https://doi.org/10.1057/ip.2014.13.

14 Tarja Cronberg, "No EU, no Iran Deal: The EU's Choice between Multilateralism and the Transatlantic Link", *The Non-Proliferation Review*, Vol. 24, No. 3–4, 2017, pp. 243–259, https://doi.org/10.1080/10736700.2018.1432321. See also, Riccardo Alcaro, *Europe and Iran's Nuclear Crisis. Lead Groups and EU Foreign Policy-Making*, Cham, Palgrave Macmillan, 2018.

15 Scott Ritter, *Dealbreaker. Donald Trump and the Unmaking of the Iran Nuclear Deal*, Atlanta, Clarity Press, 2018.

16 International Crisis Group, "Is Restoring the Iran Nuclear Deal Still Possible?", in *Middle East & North Africa Briefings*, No. 82, 12 September 2022, https://www.crisisgroup.org/node/19560.

17 Riccardo Alcaro, "Weathering the Geopolitical Storms: The Ever-elusive Success of EU Policy towards Iran", *The International Spectator*, Vol. 59, No. 1, 2024, pp. 98–119, https://doi.org/10.1080/03932729.2023.2273852.

18 Rebecca Adler-Nissen and Vincent Pouliot, "Power in Practice: Negotiating the International Intervention in Libya", *European Journal of International Relations*, Vol. 20, No. 4, 2014, pp. 889–911, https://doi.org/10.1177/1354066113512702. See also, Jesutimilehin O. Akamo, Caterina Bedin and Dario Cristiani, "The Vicious Circle of Fragmentation: The EU and the Limits of Its Approach to Libya", in *JOINT Research Papers*, No. 15, February 2023, https://www.jointproject.eu/?p=1521.

19 Caterina Bedin, Tiffany Guendouz and Agnès Levallois, "From Conflict Management to Shielding EU Stability: How Syria's Fragmentation Diverted the EU(FSP) from Action to Reaction", *The International Spectator*, Vol. 59, No. 1, 2024, pp. 79–97, https://doi.org/10.1080/03932729.2023.2277212.

20 Riccardo Alcaro, "Europe's Defence of the Iran Nuclear Deal: Less than a Success, More than a Failure", *The International Spectator*, Vol. 56, No. 1, 2021, pp. 55–72, https://doi.org/10.1080/03932729.2021.1876861.

21 Dina Esfandiary and Ariane Tabatabai, *Triple-Axis. Iran's Relations with Russia and China*, London/New York, I.B. Tauris, 2021.

22 Riccardo Alcaro, "Weathering the Geopolitical Storms: The Ever-elusive Success of EU Policy towards Iran", *The International Spectator*, Vol. 59, No. 1, 2024, pp. 98–119, https://doi.org/10.1080/03932729.2023.2273852.

23 Nicole Grajewski, "The Evolution of Russian and Iranian Cooperation in Syria", in *CSIS Analyses*, November 2021, https://www.csis.org/node/63071.

24 Zelal Başak Kizilkan, "Changing Policies of Turkey and the EU to the Syrian Conflict", *Journal of Economics and Administrative Sciences*, Vol. 33, No. 1, 2019, pp. 321–338, https://dergipark.org.tr/en/pub/atauniiibd/issue/43125/457846. See also, Caterina Bedin, Tiffany Guendouz and Agnès Levallois, "From Conflict Management to Shielding EU Stability: How Syria's Fragmentation Diverted the EU(FSP) from Action to Reaction", *The International Spectator*, Vol. 59, No. 1, 2024, pp. 79–97, https://doi.org/10.1080/03932729.2023.2277212.

25 Tarek Megerisi, "Libya's Global Civil War", in *ECFR Policy Briefs*, June 2019, https://ecfr.eu/?p=4456. See also, Jesutimilehin O. Akamo, Caterina Bedin and Dario Cristiani, "The Vicious Circle of Fragmentation: The EU and the Limits of Its Approach to Libya", in *JOINT Research Papers*, No. 15, February 2023, https://www.jointproject.eu/?p=1521.

26 Mohamed Ali Abdolgader, "Turkey, and Iran: Why Rival Powers Are Backing Ethiopia's Government", in *The New Arab*, 14 February 2022, https://www.newarab.com/node/1289463. See also, Francesca Caruso and Jesutimilehin Akamo, "EU Policy towards Ethiopia Amidst the Tigray War: The Limits of Mitigating Fragmentation", *The International Spectator*, Vol. 59, No. 1, 2024, pp. 120–139, https://doi.org/10.1080/03932729.2024.2302473.

27 Alexander Gabuev, "Russia's Support for Venezuela Has Deep Roots", in *Financial Times*, 3 February 2019, https://www.ft.com/content/0e9618e4-23c8-11e9-b20d-5376ca5216eb. See also, Ivan Garcia, "The Future of the Sino-Venezuelan Relationship: Make or Break?", in *Harvard International Review*, 22 December 2021, https://hir.harvard.edu/the-future-of-the-sino-venezuelan-relationship-make-or-break; Susanne Gratius, "The West Against the Rest? Democracy Versus Autocracy Promotion in Venezuela", *Bulletin of Latin American Research*, Vol. 41, No. 1, January 2022, pp. 141–158, https://doi.org/10.1111/blar.13243; Anna Ayuso et al., "Constraints, Dilemmas and Challenges for EU Foreign Policy in Venezuela", *The International Spectator*, Vol. 59, No. 1, 2024, pp. 140–160, https://doi.org/10.1080/03932729.2023.2289647.

28 Robert I. Rotberg (ed.), *When States Fail. Causes and Consequences*, Princeton, Princeton University Press, 2004. See also, Kristin M. Bakke, Kathleen Gallagher Cunningham and Lee J.M. Seymour, "A Plague of Initials: Fragmentation, Cohesion, and Infighting in Civil Wars", *Perspectives on Politics*, Vol. 10, No. 2, June 2012, pp. 265–283, https://doi.org/10.1017/S1537592712000667; Stephan Klingebiel, Timo Mahn and Mario Negre, "Fragmentation: A Key Concept for Development Cooperation", in Stephan Klingebiel, Timo Mahn and Mario Negre (eds), *The Fragmentation of Aid. Concepts, Measurements and Implications for Development Cooperation*, London, Palgrave Macmillan, 2016, pp. 1–18; Agnès Levallois et al., "Regional Fragmentation and EU Foreign and Security Policy", in *JOINT Research Papers*, No. 3, November 2021, https://www.jointproject.eu/?p=639.

29 Tanja A. Börzel and Thomas Risse, *Effective Governance Under Anarchy. Institutions, Legitimacy, and Social Trust in Areas of Limited Statehood*, Cambridge, Cambridge University Press, 2021.
30 Tanja A. Börzel and Thomas Risse, *Effective Governance Under Anarchy. Institutions, Legitimacy, and Social Trust in Areas of Limited Statehood*, Cambridge, Cambridge University Press, 2021.
31 Thanassis Cambanis et al. (eds), *Hybrid Actors. Armed Groups and State Fragmentation in the Middle East*, New York, The Century Foundation Press, 2019, https://tcf.org/content/report/hybrid-actors.
32 Agnès Levallois et al., "Regional Fragmentation and EU Foreign and Security Policy", in *JOINT Research Papers*, No. 3, November 2021, https://www.jointproject.eu/?p=639.
33 Kathleen Cunningham, "Understanding Fragmentation in Conflict and Its Impact on Prospects for Peace", in *Oslo Forum Papers*, No. 6, December 2016, https://hdcentre.org/?p=17920.
34 Tanja A. Börzel and Thomas Risse, *Effective Governance Under Anarchy. Institutions, Legitimacy, and Social Trust in Areas of Limited Statehood*, Cambridge, Cambridge University Press, 2021.
35 Ana E. Juncos and Steven Blockmans, "The EU's Role in Conflict Prevention and Peacebuilding: Four Key Challenges", *Global Affairs*, Vol. 4, No. 2–3, 2018, pp. 131–140, https://doi.org/10.1080/23340460.2018.1502619.
36 Sarah van Bentum et al., "How to Reduce the Impact of Internal Contestation, Regional Fragmentation and Multipolar Competition on EU Foreign and Security Policy", in *JOINT Research Papers*, No. 21, May 2023, https://www.jointproject.eu/?p=1675.
37 Sarah van Bentum et al., "How to Reduce the Impact of Internal Contestation, Regional Fragmentation and Multipolar Competition on EU Foreign and Security Policy", in *JOINT Research Papers*, No. 21, May 2023, https://www.jointproject.eu/?p=1675.
38 Caterina Bedin, Tiffany Guendouz and Agnès Levallois, "From Conflict Management to Shielding EU Stability: How Syria's Fragmentation Diverted the EU(FSP) from Action to Reaction", *The International Spectator*, Vol. 59, No. 1, 2024, pp. 79–97, https://doi.org/10.1080/03932729.2023.2277212.
39 Caterina Bedin, Tiffany Guendouz and Agnès Levallois, "From Conflict Management to Shielding EU Stability: How Syria's Fragmentation Diverted the EU(FSP) from Action to Reaction", *The International Spectator*, Vol. 59, No. 1, 2024, pp. 79–97, https://doi.org/10.1080/03932729.2023.2277212.
40 Jesutimilehin O. Akamo, Caterina Bedin and Dario Cristiani, "The Vicious Circle of Fragmentation: The EU and the Limits of Its Approach to Libya", in *JOINT Research Papers*, No. 15, February 2023, https://www.jointproject.eu/?p=1521.
41 Anna Ayuso et al., "Constraints, Dilemmas and Challenges for EU Foreign Policy in Venezuela", *The International Spectator*, Vol. 59, No. 1, 2024, pp. 140–160, https://doi.org/10.1080/03932729.2023.2289647.
42 Jesutimilehin O. Akamo, Caterina Bedin and Dario Cristiani, "The Vicious Circle of Fragmentation: The EU and the Limits of Its Approach to

Libya", in *JOINT Research Papers*, No. 15, February 2023, https://www.jointproject.eu/?p=1521.

43 Michela Ceccorulli and Fabrizio Coticchia, "'I'll Take Two.' Migration, Terrorism, and the Italian Military Engagement in Niger and Libya", *Journal of Modern Italian Studies*, Vol. 25, No. 2, 2020, pp. 174–196, https://doi.org/10.1080/1354571X.2020.1723291.

44 Andrew Lebovich and Tarek Megerisi, "France's Strongman Strategy in the Sahel", in *ECFR Commentaries*, 8 March 2019, https://ecfr.eu/?p=8011.

45 Rosanne Anholt and Giulia Sinatti, "Under the Guise of Resilience: The EU Approach to Migration and Forced Displacement in Jordan and Lebanon", *Contemporary Security Policy*, Vol. 41, No. 2, 2020, pp. 311–335, https://doi.org/10.1080/13523260.2019.1698182. See also, Marc Pierini, "In Search of an EU Role in the Syrian War", in *Carnegie Reports*, August 2016, https://carnegieendowment.org/publications/64352.

46 Francesca Caruso and Jesutimilehin Akamo, "EU Policy towards Ethiopia Amidst the Tigray War: The Limits of Mitigating Fragmentation", *The International Spectator*, Vol. 59, No. 1, 2024, pp. 120–139, https://doi.org/10.1080/03932729.2024.2302473.

47 Francesca Caruso and Jesutimilehin Akamo, "EU Policy towards Ethiopia Amidst the Tigray War: The Limits of Mitigating Fragmentation", *The International Spectator*, Vol. 59, No. 1, 2024, pp. 120–139, https://doi.org/10.1080/03932729.2024.2302473.

48 Kristi Raik et al., "Not Yet Fit for the World: Piecemeal Buildup of EU Military, Cyber and Intelligence Assets", in *JOINT Research Papers*, No. 4, November 2021, https://www.jointproject.eu/?p=648.

49 Wolfram Lacher, *Libya's Fragmentation. Structure and Process in Violent Conflict*, London, I.B. Tauris, 2020; Jesutimilehin O. Akamo, Caterina Bedin and Dario Cristiani, "The Vicious Circle of Fragmentation: The EU and the Limits of Its Approach to Libya", in *JOINT Research Papers*, No. 15, February 2023, https://www.jointproject.eu/?p=1521.

50 Christopher Phillips, "The Civil War in Syria: The Variety of Opposition to the Syrian Regime", in *IEMed Mediterranean Yearbook 2013*, pp. 24–29, https://www.iemed.org/publication/the-civil-war-in-syria-the-variety-of-opposition-to-the-syrian-regime.

51 Liesbet Hooghe and Gary Marks, "A Postfunctionalist Theory of European Integration: From Permissive Consensus to Constraining Dissensus", *British Journal of Political Science*, Vol. 39, No. 1, 2009, pp. 1–23, https://doi.org/10.1017/S0007123408000409.

52 Patrick Müller, Karolina Pomorska and Ben Tonra, "The Domestic Challenge to EU Foreign Policymaking: From Europeanisation to de-Europeanisation?", *Journal of European Integration*, Vol. 43, No. 5, 2021, pp. 519–534, https://doi.org/10.1080/07036337.2021.1927015.

53 Pieter de Wilde and Hans J. Trenz, "Denouncing European Integration: Euroscepticism as Polity Contestation", *European Journal of Social Theory*, Vol. 15, No. 4, 2012, pp. 537–554, https://doi.org/10.1177/1368431011432968. See also, Rosa Balfour (ed.), *Europe's Troublemakers. The Populist Challenge to Foreign Policy*, Brussels, European Policy Centre, 2016, https://www.epc.eu/en/Publications/~257da8; Franziska Petri, Elodie Thevenin and

Lins Liedlbauer, "Contestation of European Union Foreign Policy: Causes, Modes and Effects", *Global Affairs*, Vol. 6, No. 4–5, 2020, pp. 323–328, https://doi.org/10.1080/23340460.2020.1863159.

54 Joanna Dyduch and Patrick Müller, "Populism Meets EU Foreign Policy: The De-Europeanization of Poland's Foreign Policy toward the Israeli-Palestinian Conflict", *Journal of European Integration*, Vol. 43, No. 5, 2021, pp. 569–586, https://doi.org/10.1080/07036337.2021.1927010.

55 Sandra Destradi, David Cadier and Johannes Plagemann, "Populism and Foreign Policy: A Research Agenda (Introduction)", *Comparative European Politics*, Vol. 19, No. 6, 2021, pp. 663–682, https://doi.org/10.1057/s41295-021-00255-4.

56 Katja Biedenkopf, Oriol Costa and Magdalena Góra, "Introduction: Shades of Contestation and Politicisation of CFSP", *European Security*, Vol. 30, No. 3, 2021, pp. 325–343, https://doi.org/10.1080/09662839.2021.1964473

57 Riccardo Alcaro and Hylke Dijkstra, "Re-imagining EU Foreign and Security Policy in a Complex and Contested World", *The International Spectator*, Vol. 59, No. 1, 2024, pp. 1–18, https://doi.org/10.1080/03932729.2024.2304028.

58 Patrick Müller, Karolina Pomorska and Ben Tonra, "The Domestic Challenge to EU Foreign Policymaking: From Europeanisation to de-Europeanisation?", *Journal of European Integration*, Vol. 43, No. 5, 2021, pp. 519–534, https://doi.org/10.1080/07036337.2021.1927015. See also, Marianna Lovato et al., "The Internal Contestation of EU Foreign and Security Policy", in *JOINT Research Papers*, No. 1, September 2021, https://www.jointproject.eu/?p=516.

59 Sarah van Bentum et al., "How to Reduce the Impact of Internal Contestation, Regional Fragmentation and Multipolar Competition on EU Foreign and Security Policy", in *JOINT Research Papers*, No. 21, May 2023, https://www.jointproject.eu/?p=1675.

60 Sarah van Bentum et al., "How to Reduce the Impact of Internal Contestation, Regional Fragmentation and Multipolar Competition on EU Foreign and Security Policy", in *JOINT Research Papers*, No. 21, May 2023, https://www.jointproject.eu/?p=1675.

61 Ioannis Armakolas and James Ker-Lindsay (eds), *The Politics of Recognition and Engagement. EU Member State Relations with Kosovo*, Cham, Palgrave Macmillan, 2020.

62 Pol Bargués et al., "Engagement against All Odds? Navigating Member States' Contestation of EU Policy on Kosovo", *The International Spectator*, Vol. 59, No. 1, 2024, pp. 19–38, https://doi.org/10.1080/03932729.2023.2295893.

63 Sarah van Bentum et al., "How to Reduce the Impact of Internal Contestation, Regional Fragmentation and Multipolar Competition on EU Foreign and Security Policy", in *JOINT Research Papers*, No. 21, May 2023, https://www.jointproject.eu/?p=1675.

64 Anna Ayuso, Marianne Riddervold and Elsa Lilja Gunnarsdottir, "The EU Trapped in the Venezuelan Labyrinth: Challenges to Finding a Way Out", in *JOINT Research Papers*, No. 18, February 2023, https://www.jointproject.eu/?p=1550.

65 Anna Ayuso et al., "Constraints, Dilemmas and Challenges for EU Foreign Policy in Venezuela", *The International Spectator*, Vol. 59, No. 1, 2024, pp. 140–160, https://doi.org/10.1080/03932729.2023.2289647.
66 Raffaella A. Del Sarto, "Stuck in the Logic of Oslo: Europe and the Israeli-Palestinian Conflict", *The Middle East Journal*, Vol. 73, No. 3, 2019, pp. 376–396, https://doi.org/10.3751/73.3.12; Sinem Akgül-Açıkmeşe and Soli Özel, "EU Policy towards the Israel-Palestine Conflict: The Limitations of Mitigation Strategies", *The International Spectator*, Vol. 59, No. 1, 2024, pp. 59–78, https://doi.org/10.1080/03932729.2024.2309664.
67 International Crisis Group, "Realigning European Policy toward Palestine with Ground Realities", in *Middle East Reports*, No. 237, 23 August 2022, https://www.crisisgroup.org/node/19491; Sinem Akgül-Açıkmeşe and Soli Özel, "EU Policy towards the Israel-Palestine Conflict: The Limitations of Mitigation Strategies", *The International Spectator*, Vol. 59, No. 1, 2024, pp. 59–78, https://doi.org/10.1080/03932729.2024.2309664.
68 Joanna Dyduch, "The Visegrád Group's Policy towards Israel", in *SWP Comments*, No. 54, December 2018, https://www.swp-berlin.org/en/publication/the-visegrad-groups-policy-towards-israel.
69 Zeev Sternhell, "Why Benjamin Netanyahu Loves the European Far-Right", in *Foreign Policy*, 24 February 2019, http://bit.ly/2Viu1we. See also, Joshua Shanes, "Netanyahu, Orbán, and the Resurgence of Antisemitism: Lessons of the Last Century", *Shofar*, Vol. 37, No. 1, Spring 2019, pp. 108–120, https://doi.org/10.5703/shofar.37.1.0108.
70 Christian Lamour, "Orbán Placed in Europe: Ukraine, Russia and the Radical-Right Populist Heartland", in *Geopolitics*, Vol. 29, No. 4, 2023, pp. 1297–1323, https://doi.org/10.1080/14650045.2023.2241825.
71 Kristi Raik et al., "EU Policy towards Ukraine: Entering Geopolitical Competition over European Order", in *The International Spectator*, Vol. 59, No. 1 2024, pp. 39–58, https://doi.org/10.1080/03932729.2023.2296576.
72 Sarah van Bentum et al., "How to Reduce the Impact of Internal Contestation, Regional Fragmentation and Multipolar Competition on EU Foreign and Security Policy", in *JOINT Research Papers*, No. 21, May 2023, https://www.jointproject.eu/?p=1675.
73 Pol Bargués et al., "Time to Re-engage with Kosovo and Serbia: Strengthening EU Foreign and Security Policy amidst Internal Contestation", in *JOINT Research Papers*, No. 12, December 2022, https://www.jointproject.eu/?p=1459.
74 Beken Saatçioğlu, "The EU's Response to the Syrian Refugee Crisis: A Battleground among Many Europes", *European Politics and Society*, Vol. 22, No. 5, 2021, pp. 808–823, https://doi.org/10.1080/23745118.2020.1842693.
75 Caterina Bedin, Tiffany Guendouz and Agnès Levallois, "From Conflict Management to Shielding EU Stability: How Syria's Fragmentation Diverted the EU(FSP) from Action to Reaction", *The International Spectator*, Vol. 59, No. 1, 2024, pp. 79–97, https://doi.org/10.1080/03932729.2023.2277212.
76 Kristi Raik et al., "EU Policy towards Ukraine: Entering Geopolitical Competition over European Order", *The International Spectator*, Vol. 59, No. 1, 2024, pp. 39–58, https://doi.org/10.1080/03932729.2023.2296576.

77 Deborah Feldman, "Germany Is a Good Place to Be Jewish. Unless, Like Me, You're a Jew Who Criticises Israel", in *The Guardian*, 13 November 2023, https://www.theguardian.com/p/paj6c.

78 Kristina Kausch, "A Decade of Deadlock. The EU's Shipwreck on Palestine Embodies the EU's Blockade Problem", in *JOINT Briefs*, No. 33, March 2024, https://www.jointproject.eu/?p=2011.

79 Alessia Melcangi and Karim Mezran, "Truly a Proxy War? Militias, Institutions and External Actors in Libya between Limited Statehood and Rentier State", *The International Spectator*, Vol. 57, No. 4, 2022, pp. 121–138, https://www.tandfonline.com/doi/full/10.1080/03932729.2022.2061225

4 The strengths and limits of relational power Europe

The challenging context of EUFSP described in Chapter 3 weighs heavily on the EU's ability to meet its goals for conflict management and resolution. Great power rivalry and the fragmentation of states and regions generate multiple constraints, while multi-source internal contestation, interplaying with the systemic factors, adds more sticks to an already slow wheel. While the previous chapter brought to the fore the 'dependence' element nested in the relational nature of EUFSP, in this chapter the focus is on the 'resilience' dimension of it, that is, on how the EU navigated the contextual constraints.

Underperformance – by the EU as well as its member states – generally fuelled downbeat assessments. The feeling that Europe was not up to the task was as shared in the policymaking community as it was in the research world. In the foreword to the Strategic Compass, HRVP Borrell invoked "a quantum leap forward on security and defence", which required additional investment, greater coordination and cooperation and a power-oriented strategic mindset.[1] Commenting on such ambitions, policy experts pointed to the shortcomings in EUFSP structures, deficiencies in terms of coordination and coherence across policy areas as well as a fragmented discourse and ambiguity in communication.[2] Academics contended that, in spite of sustained efforts at greater policy cohesion especially in support of Ukraine, the EU's foreign and security policy capacity was "residual",[3] strategic autonomy a "pipe dream" and the 2022 Strategic Compass "already obsolete".[4] Such evaluations tend to describe an EUFSP that invariably stumbles, and falls, into the "expectation-capability gap" that has been a structural feature of it since its inception.[5] These assessments start off, implicitly if not explicitly, from an inside-out understanding of the EU; what informs them is the suboptimal institutional set-up of the EU, and of EUFSP, in particular.

DOI: 10.4324/9781003559467-5

We do not disagree with the observation that the EU's foreign and security policy record is mixed at best, and especially underwhelming when the focus is narrowed down to crises and conflicts. There are very few, if any, success stories in this regard.[6] However, in our view an assessment of EUFSP based on its nature as an intergovernmental-supranational hybrid is necessary but not sufficient. Context – both systemic and domestic – is equally important in constituting the EU's capacity for actorness in international security and consequently in informing an assessment of EUFSP. Therefore, in this chapter we do not so much focus on what the EU lacked in terms of decision-making procedures, institutions and resources, as on how it handled the contextual challenges when dealing with conflicts and crises. Recent studies describe the panoply of strategies, tactics and practices that the EU uses to deal with the contextual challenges as "mitigation measures".[7] Such measures may be deliberate and signal strategic behaviour on the part of the EU or may develop over time surreptitiously, on the back of past experiences and path dependencies in a complex process of adaptation to external and domestic pressures.

The modes of handling the contextual challenges emanate almost naturally from a process-based and multi-dimensional EUFSP. The EU entertains different forms of engagement with external players (be they international organisations, great powers, regional or local actors), deploys instruments from policy areas disciplined by distinct institutional and decision-making procedures and comprises multiple actors, that is, common institutions and member states.[8] This multi-dimensionality turns the making of EUFSP into a complex and cumbersome exercise, but it also provides for options that national foreign policies lack. Critically, this multi-dimensional and process-based foreign policy enabled the EU to continuously adapt and cope with the effects arising from the contextual factors.

The EU's in-built drive towards initiating multilateral processes within international institutions and ad hoc formats helped deflecting multipolar pressures on the EU.[9] The multi-sectoral nature of EUFSP allowed EU institutions and member states to approach crises and conflicts incrementally and asymmetrically through decoupling and selective engagement.[10] Finally, the multi-actor character of EUFSP was used to bypass internal contestation challenges – in particular, through the delegation of conflict management responsibilities to EU institutions or select groups of member states.[11] An analytical framework that focuses on the EU's modes of handling the contextual challenges is a heuristic lens through which EUFSP action in conflict management can be evaluated.[12]

This chapter explores the resilience dimension of relational power Europe. We first examine the tactics that the EU and member states use to address the contextual challenges separately, one section each. In the conclusion, we explain how this process is more complex, as challenges and responses are deeply interconnected.

Handling multipolar competition

In Chapter 3, we saw how multipolar competition lays bare some structural limitations of the EU and its member states, spanning their relative military weakness, the erosion of multilateral governance and the greater ability of crisis and conflict actors to resist the allure of European incentives or circumvent European coercive measures. It is mostly against this backdrop that the aspiration to transform the EU into a geopolitical pole has grown. That aspiration has been realised only very limitedly, though. When looking at international crises and even more so at conflicts, a frequent observation is that the Union is less powerful and less influential than other 'poles'.[13] Still, we argue, the EU tries and sometimes is able to handle multipolar rivalries and their multifarious effects. The main instrument that the EU relies on to do that is multilateralisation.

Multilateralisation is about the construction of problems in accordance with international law as well as the development of collaborative crisis management regimes. Multilateralisation is thus about how crises and conflicts are addressed in both discourse and practice.

So, for instance, the EU framed cooperation with Southeast Asian countries on (amongst others) maritime security, biodiversity and fisheries as a means to strengthen a rules-based governance system in the South China Sea, where China's territorial claims fuelled strong antagonism with the United States.[14] Another case in which the EU championed multilateral norms with a view to moderate geopolitical rivalries was the effort by France, Germany and the United Kingdom (E3), together with the HRVP, to address the dispute over Iran's nuclear programme.[15] From the start of this long-lasting crisis, the E3 and the HRVP – or E3/EU, as they were formally known – lured Iran into nuclear talks by framing the problem as being about an unlawful behaviour (Iran's non-compliance with its international non-proliferation obligations) rather than the anti-Western ideological orientation of the Iranian regime.[16] In so doing, the E3/EU helped an initially hostile United States to engage directly with Iran and eventually sign the JCPOA or Iran nuclear deal in 2015.[17] This process spanned nearly a decade and involved not so much a reconfiguration of United States-Iran antagonism as the delimitation of a normative space with which both Washington and Tehran could relate.[18] The E3 and HRVP continued to follow the same normative-driven approach in the years that followed the United States' abrupt unilateral withdrawal from the nuclear deal under President Donald Trump.[19] Even if ultimately unsuccessful in saving the JCPOA, the European approach contributed to reduce the impact of geopolitical and ideological rivalry on the management of the nuclear dossier for many years.

The EU also pursues inclusive ad hoc coalitions focussing on individual crises or conflicts. Because they involve a limited number of countries, these groups are discussed in the literature under the "minilateralism" heading.[20] These minilateral groupings have the advantage of sharing out responsibility for crisis management with relevant actors, including local and regional ones. More importantly, they extend ownership of the management of specific crises to countries that otherwise could have a greater interest in spoiling crisis management and resolution.

A case in point is the early support that EU member states gave to a United Nations-led initiative on Syria's civil war, the so-called Geneva process. The initiative sought (in vain) to bridge the divide between the United States and Russia, which headed the camps of opponents and defenders of the Assad regime, respectively.[21] Another example of minilateralism can be seen in the EU engagement with Venezuela. In 2019, the HRVP spearheaded an International Contact Group comprising a number of EU and Latin American states, which took on themselves to monitor the situation in Venezuela and coordinate positions on how democracy could be restored there.[22] While the group did not achieve substantial results, its ostensibly neutral position helped the EU gain a degree of access to the Venezuelan government. It also lent some credibility to the EU's support for a Norway-led, Mexico-based mediation attempt in which Russia acted as the informal guarantor of the Maduro government.[23]

It is again the nuclear dispute with Iran that offers an exemplary case of how minilateralism could sustain crisis resolution efforts while containing multipolar rivalries. The JCPOA was a multilateral deal signed by all five permanent members of the Security Council, as well as Germany and the HRVP, which had for years managed the Iranian nuclear dossier within an ad hoc contact group that had originated from a European initiative (so much so that the official name of the group was E3/EU+3). The inclusion of China and Russia in the group disincentivised them to act as spoilers, in spite of the fact that in the early 2010s the relationship of both countries with the United States and Europe was deteriorating rapidly (especially after Russia annexed Crimea in 2014).[24] The group continued to function even after the United States' withdrawal from the nuclear agreement, only dissipating when Russia's second, large-scale invasion of Ukraine in 2022 resulted in an almost total breakdown of its relations with Western countries.[25]

The multilateralisation pursued by the EU and its member states can also be exclusive rather than inclusive and 'geopolitically' oriented rather than driven by norms. This happens when EU institutions and member states view coalitions with allies and partners not so much as a tool for reducing multipolar competition but as a lever to increase their influence over rival countries or conflict parties themselves.

An example of strategic partnering is the EU's approach to geopolitical tensions in the Indo-Pacific. The EU has taken steps to meet US expectations of greater transatlantic coordination on China-related issues, especially on the need to reduce vulnerabilities to China-controlled supply chains – or de-risk, as it has become common to say. At the same time, the Union has sought tighter economic and political ties with a number of regional countries (including Japan, South Korea, Australia, New Zealand, Malaysia, Thailand and Singapore) in an attempt to have the Indo-Pacific multipolar game at least partly reflect its own normative, strategic and commercial preferences.[26]

The most obvious example of how the EU seeks to gain influence over rivals through coalition-building with third parties is the war in Ukraine.[27] Engagement with the United States regularly occurred at multiple levels: the Ramstein format for coordinating military supplies to Kyiv (a mechanism transferred to NATO in July 2024); the bilateral dialogue on sanctions (started well before the invasion); and actions within the G7 on technically complex measures, such as the freezing of the Russian Central Bank's foreign reserves (and their requisition and use to support Ukraine's defence and reconstruction) and the establishment of a price cap on Russia's oil exports. These partnerships, occurring within the traditional Western circles of NATO, EU-US formats and the G7, were so critical to the EU's ability to support Kyiv and pressure Moscow that they should in fact be regarded as enablers of the EU's overall strategic involvement in the Ukraine war.[28] Without these coalitions, the EU and its member states would have been forced to revise their objectives as their leverage over Ukraine and especially Russia would diminish considerably.

These various measures of multilateralisation shore up EU crisis management capacities, while mitigating the strains of multipolar competition. The relative modesty of European military capabilities becomes less of a problem if rival 'poles' develop shared sensibilities in crisis resolution through inclusive ad hoc groupings. When this proves impossible, strategic partnering with the United States and other like-minded countries partly compensates for the limitations of European hard power. The EU's capacity to contribute to multilateral coalition-building is obviously meant to offset the hollowing out of international institutions. Strong emphasis on international law pushes rival powers to compete not just through their material strengths but also for global legitimacy through normative claims. In addition, inclusive minilateral groups can reinforce multilateral institutions and regimes; the E3/EU+3 Iran group, for instance, gained much of its legitimacy from being officially sanctioned by successive United Nations Security Council resolutions, while it also empowered the International Atomic Energy Agency and reinforced the authority of the Nuclear Non-Proliferation Treaty. Finally, multilateral frameworks amplify the incisiveness of both EU incentives and restrictions, thus reducing the room for seeking alternatives of conflict and crisis parties.

Underlying the EU's preference for multilateralisation is the fact that, with few exceptions, the Union tends to approach crises and conflicts as transnational problems rather than arenas of geopolitical confrontation for which it is ill-equipped institutionally and in terms of resources. Convergence with the United States (as well as other like-minded countries) is critical in this regard because it strengthens EU efforts to multilateralise crisis and conflict management. In this sense, Atlanticism is functional to multilateralism as an antidote to multipolar competition. However, when multilateralisation is impracticable – as in the case of Ukraine – the EU can only fall back on its partnership with the United States to sustain an unavoidable geopolitical contest. Here, Atlanticism is the alternative to multilateralism.

None of the above implies that multilateralisation enables the EU to overcome fully the constraints imposed by multipolar competition. In fact, these measures are mostly about mitigation and, unsurprisingly, EUFSP's successes are rarer than failures. Even when they occur, such successes tend to be temporary – all the benefits that multilateralisation brought to the EU's handling of the Iranian nuclear issue, for instance, eventually vanished under the strains of geopolitical rivalries, as recalled in Chapter 3. Still, the analytically relevant point is that the EU deploys multilateralisation as a means to be resilient to a context marred by power rivalry. Ultimately, successes and failures in facing multipolar rivalries are a reflection of whether EU institutions and member states maximise the potential of multilateralisation measures.

Handling regional fragmentation

In Chapter 3, we discussed how fragmentation of states and regions invariably leads to a proliferation of conflict actors and a multiplication of challenges. European policymakers, who are often expected to accord preference to different (even conflicting) priorities, lose focus on the general picture and consequently EUFSP becomes itself fragmented. Still, this constraint does not mean that the EU is inactive.

When fragmentation is acute, the Union and its member states try to deconstruct highly political issues, over which arrangements with conflict parties is seemingly impossible, into technical issues where some form of understanding is more realistic.[29] The EU does so by decoupling – that is, temporarily separating – particularly problematic issues from the other tasks of conflict management or, alternatively, it engages conflict parties selectively on specific issues only.

Decoupling was most prominently used in the peacebuilding process between Kosovo and Serbia.[30] The enlargement process provided a unified policy framework for the EU's relations with both conflict parties, yet the most intractable issue, the recognition of Kosovo's independence, was temporarily set aside while progress was pursued on other dossiers (for instance, visa facilitation). The decoupling of the final status issue was meant to make room for embedding the conflict parties into EU rules and institutions as much as possible before the EU could go back to link its own relations with Serbia and Kosovo to the final status issue, as accession of either party could only happen if a final settlement on Kosovo's status were reached.[31]

Decoupling helped unblock EUFSP in other instances, including the EU's Ukraine policy prior to 2022. France and Germany pursued mediation over the Donbas – Ukraine's eastern region where Russia had fomented a low intensity war since spring 2014 – on a separate track, the so-called Normandy framework. Meanwhile, EU institutions and member states continued to work towards the democratic and economic stabilisation of Ukraine.[32] Decoupling was meant to prevent the Donbas issue from engulfing the whole EU-Ukraine cooperation agenda (on this, it succeeded) and from blocking the overall EU-Russia relationship (on this, it failed spectacularly).[33]

The EU resorted to decoupling also in its approach towards Venezuela. It put humanitarian aid and election monitoring on a separate track from its main policy of facilitating national reconciliation and the restoration of democratic practices in the country. The EU depoliticised the provision of aid to Venezuelans by channelling it through the United Nations, thus avoiding that it could become hostage to the clash between regime and opposition.[34] Furthermore, it crafted an EU observation mission of local elections in 2021 in ways with which both regime and opposition could be comfortable. The former saw the mission as a form of international legitimation and the latter as an instrument to further expose the Maduro regime's anti-democratic practices.[35] Decoupling these two issues from the higher-level interaction on national reconciliation allowed for modest but concrete results, such as alleviating refugees' suffering and gathering valuable information on the situation inside the country. The idea was that they would help build trust (of the EU and between the conflict parties) and thus contribute to national reconciliation indirectly.[36]

Decoupling is supposed to be temporary, meaning that the holistic logic underlying the integrated approach is not abandoned. There are circumstances, however, when EU institutions and member states adopt a different approach and deliberately pursue conditional interaction with crisis or conflict actors on selected issues only.

The E3/EU's attempt to ensure that Iran's nuclear programme would not be diverted to military uses rigidly followed this logic of selective engagement. Persuaded that, if left unaddressed, the nuclear dispute would destabilise the Middle East and jeopardise the international non-proliferation regime, the Europeans insisted for years on insulating the nuclear talks. In particular, they de-linked the nuclear file from Iran's support for its network of nonstate allies in Iraq, Lebanon and Yemen (and Syria, though there Iran supported the central government too). The prioritisation and compartmentalisation of the nuclear issue derived from the latter's geopolitical magnitude. Solving it was an end in itself. However, the Europeans also counted on the possibility that success on the nuclear front could facilitate interaction on other regional issues.[37] While Iran made no appreciable change to its regional policy during the diplomatic process that culminated in the deal (2003–2015) and for as long as the JCPOA remained in place (2016–2018), it did become markedly more aggressive regionally after the United States' withdrawal from the deal, thus retroactively proving the validity of the EU's compartmentalisation tactic.

Selective engagement can also be tailored to more limited actions on emergencies or politically less salient issues when higher-level interactions remain stalled or when the EU has little leverage to advance a conflict resolution agenda. This is the case, for instance, of the EU's financial assistance and capacity-building initiatives in the Palestinian territories, which were supposed to strengthen the institutional clout of the Palestinian Authority.[38] In theory, these measures were included in a broader conflict resolution framework: a stronger and more efficient Palestinian Authority was supposed to become a catalyst for greater unity amongst rival Palestinian factions and therefore a stronger negotiating counterpart of Israel.[39] Still narrower forms of selective engagement take place when the EU deliberately restricts interaction with conflict actors to a minimum. A case in point was the EU's policy of providing Syrians with humanitarian aid without channelling it through the Assad regime.[40]

These strategies, tactics and practices are meant to mitigate the effects on EUFSP of regional fragmentation that we identified in Chapter 3. Selective engagement is a response to the 'interlocutor selection' problem. It works best when the EU and the external interlocutor can isolate an issue of common concern from regional dynamics of divisions. For example, compartmentalising the nuclear issue allowed the E3/EU to remain engaged with Iran in spite of the latter's destabilising policies in the Middle East (as well as its abysmal human rights record).

Selective engagement can also ease the tension between conflict management goals and other issues of concern to which the EU and its member states accord greater preference. It provides for policy options that, while marginal to conflict management, at least allow the EU and its member states to remain engaged in it (examples include the provision of humanitarian aid in Syria or the technical assistance to the Palestinian Authority).

Selective engagement offers some modest advantages also with regard to the difficulty of generating contextual knowledge of conflicts or crises (a final challenge emanating from fragmented areas). The deployment of civilian CSDP missions decoupled from higher-level conflict management efforts, even for limited purposes such as election observation, border monitoring or capacity-building, contribute to gathering valuable information on the ground.

Still, none of the above-mentioned cases should be considered a success conflict resolution story (of the EU's or anyone else's).[41] Perhaps even more than multipolar competition, fragmentation dynamics make crisis and conflict management extremely challenging. Decoupling tactics have generated some benefits but have not brought the EU closer to the facilitation of peace settlements. At times, these may even have contributed to the perpetuation of conflict, as in the cases of pre-2022 Ukraine or Israel-Palestine. Narrower selective engagements are by definition residual policy actions, in that they only provide some mitigation to the worst effects of fragmentation (such as humanitarian crises), but do not in themselves contribute to overcoming deeper logics of fragmentation. Selective engagement, in its multiple variants, is not to be understood as an optimal solution to crises or conflicts, but as a means to creatively expand the EU's options in ways that are out of reach for individual member states.

In handling regional fragmentation, the EU acts with elasticity and pragmatism. When the EU is unable to engage in higher-level political interactions with conflict parties, it can still activate a panoply of 'low-politics' assets (such election monitoring, humanitarian aid, etc.) to at least establish a presence in the conflict area and keep channels of communication with conflict parties open: it is thus elastic in the sense that the panoply of instruments at its disposal allows it to 'bounce back' into action when high-level political engagement is impractical. Even when it does manage to engage conflict parties in high-level political talks, the EU can only act based on hard trade-offs between its normative and strategic goals and the domestic priorities of its member states; its foreign policy in fragmented areas is therefore invariably informed with pragmatism.

Handling internal contestation

In Chapter 3, we saw that intra-EU contestation on how to manage crises or conflicts has multiple origins. Member states act on the basis of domestically construed interests that reflect their history, society and political experience. It is to be expected that they feel the imperative to defend vigorously such interests at the EU level, even if that contrasts with or undermines broader conflict management goals. But contestation of EUFSP may also result from party ideology or from a perceived electoral advantage. Finally, it can reflect widespread trends in the public opinion that cross party lines and which national political elites are unwilling to challenge.

The lack of consensus among member states is traditionally considered the main weakness of the EU's foreign and security policy. It is no surprise that for decades policymakers and scholars have struggled to consider the EU as a collective and have advocated a 'single voice' strategy.[42] Much of this logic informed the Lisbon Treaty, the strengthening of the position of the HRVP and the creation of the EEAS. Nevertheless, the problem of a lack of 'single voice' has not gone away and EU member states continue to disagree and dilute, slow down or even paralyse collective action. This said, over time EU member states have found ways to sidestep internal disagreements by making use of the EU's multi-actorness, giving rise to a 'polymorphic' actor, that is, a collective non-homogeneous actor. Scholars have taken notice and construed a multi-actor EUFSP as an articulation of the broader trend of 'differentiated integration' or 'differentiated cooperation'.[43]

There are, of course, several ways in which intra-EU divisions can be overcome. The most common – in fact, the standard – method for addressing internal contestation revolves around deliberation and negotiation, whereby member states engage with one another on the basis of arguments and reciprocal concessions. Deliberation is critical to problem framing, as EU member states achieve little if they fail to see a crisis or conflict through the same lens. Generally, deliberation is proactive and inclusive, as member state governments strive for consensus. Still, there are occasions in which unanimous agreement on problem framing is impossible, and choices on policy formulation and implementation are forced upon individual member states through a combination of concessions and peer pressure. The exemptions from the EU's oil embargo on Russia granted to a few member states in 2022 are a case in point. Another one is Hungary's capitulation in early 2024 on the authorisation of a 50-billion-euro aid package to Ukraine over a four-year period in the face of intense pressure from the other 26 members.

However, deliberation and negotiation can and do fail on a regular basis and yet we observe that paralysis or common denominator positions are not the only outcome of stalemate. Over the years EU member states have made use of delegation as a way out of the impasse brought about by internal contestation. Delegation involves the transfer, which may be temporary or partial, of specific dossiers to EU institutions or to groups of member states, relieving member states of tasks which they are reluctant to take up.

One way in which delegation occurs is when member states give EU institutions (or even individual member states) responsibility for dealing with a crisis within a mandate over which they maintain control. This form of direct delegation allows member states to temporarily abdicate the responsibility of closely following the management of a conflict. In so doing, governments that would have a strong interest in contesting EU policy for domestic reasons escape whatever political harm they might incur if they were to act directly.[44]

This tactic was used in the Kosovo-Serbia dossier, which was largely managed by the HRVP autonomously – with the Commission providing a supporting role and the Council general oversight. All policies over which the HRVP and the Commission presided – the rule of law EULEX mission in Kosovo, the Belgrade-Pristina Dialogue, the enlargement process, and others such as visa liberalisation – were framed as 'neutral' to the state of Kosovo as an independent country, a necessary concession to the five member states that did not recognise its sovereignty but were nonetheless interested in solving its dispute with Serbia.[45]

Other cases of formal delegation, albeit for narrower tasks, concerned Venezuela and the Israeli-Palestinian conflict. The ideological divisions that prevented unanimous agreement on the recognition of Venezuela's opposition leader as the legitimate interim president in 2019 did not stop EU member states from entrusting the HRVP with conflict management tasks.[46] In particular, the HRVP and the EEAS coordinated the work of the International Contact Group (of which eight EU states were also members) to facilitate national reconciliation talks. The case of Israel-Palestine is more complex. Powerful domestic constituencies across Europe opposing any form of pressure on Israel long prevented the EU from any sustained diplomatic engagement beyond a rhetorical commitment to the two-state solution. Member states found a way to remain (barely) involved in the conflict through the delegation to EU institutions of the provision of financial and technical assistance to the Palestinian Authority.[47]

Delegation can also occur in informal ways, not so much on a mandate but on ex-post, tacit approval. This occurs when a group of member states, acting in coordination with each other and sometimes involving EU institutions, take the initiative and engage in conflict or crisis management. In so doing, they create momentum behind their policy line that is strong enough for the other member states to opt for acquiescence to the group's leadership rather than opposition to it. After all, the responsibility for failure lies with the group. In addition, the outsiders retain some control over the group's action if crisis management requires, as it invariably does, the activation of EU tools for which unanimity is necessary (for instance, the adoption of sanctions).[48]

An example of lead groups is the Contact Group for the Balkans. This comprised the United States and (for a time) Russia as well as four EU member states, namely France, Germany, Italy and the United Kingdom, and benefitted from technical support from the European Commission.[49] The group drove EU policy towards Bosnia-Herzegovina and Kosovo for years, facilitating the creation of intra-EU consensus for extending to all Balkan countries the promise of EU membership (an option that could otherwise have become the source of insurmountable divisions within the EU).[50]

Another notable instance is the E3/EU Iran team. Thanks to a remarkable capacity for initiative, the group rapidly gained control of the EU's Iran policy.[51] The group managed to do so because it prioritised the nuclear dispute, over which intra-EU contestation was minimal, rather than other issues such as trade, human rights and regional security, on which member states held different views.[52] A further example worth mentioning is the Normandy contact group, in which France and Germany tried to mediate a resolution to the war in the Donbas between 2015 and 2022. The Normandy format is especially interesting because it was never popular within the EU and yet it contributed to shape EU policy – the retention or lifting of sanctions was linked to the results of the Normandy process.[53] Even lesser actions such as the joint visits by Italy's Prime Minister Giorgia Meloni and Commission President von der Leyen to Tunisia in 2023 (alongside Dutch Prime Minister Mark Rutte) and Egypt in 2024 (with Belgium's Alexander de Croo) to strike border control deals can be put into this category.

Even when they hold divergent views, EU member state governments generally have an interest in finding some common ground. Contestation has its shades of grey and EU member states have learned that, at times, it can be bypassed through delegation. The leveraging of common institutions and lead groups increases the EU's capacity to deal with crises and conflicts more extensively than what a policy based exclusively on universal agreement would allow for. It is on this basis that we consider the characterisation of the EU as a collective actor in international security legitimate. However, it is appropriate to qualify it with the adjective 'polymorphic' to emphasise its non-homogeneous and multi-actor nature. This, moreover, implies that the capacity for collective action in crises and conflicts expressed by the lead groups is not structural but contingent on ad hoc factors, namely the capacity for initiative of the groups' insiders and their ability to find working syntheses with the group's outsiders.

Conclusion

This chapter has analysed how the EU and its member states handled the effects emanating from contextual factors when addressing crises and conflicts. We have shown how the EU relied on forms of multilateralisation to handle multipolar pressures; how it dealt with specific issues selectively while neglecting more contentious ones in an attempt to overcome problems associated with regional fragmentation; and how it used delegation to EU institutions or lead groups of member states to sidestep internal contestation. Contrary to widespread views that see paralysis, incapacity and feeble actorness in EUFSP, we have provided a framework to understand how the EU pursues its objectives of conflict management creatively and uniquely, amidst a global context of growing complexity and interstate competition.

Just as the contextual factors intersect with one another, so the three modes of handling them do not speak one-to-one with individual constraints, but can simultaneously address challenges emanating from the other ones too. To illustrate, multilateralisation can reduce the spillovers of regional fragmentation by generating cooperative multipolar interactions at the regional level. Because it carries added political weight and greater international legitimacy, multilateralisation is also effective in tempering intra-EU contestation. Selective engagement, which we have analysed in relation to the challenges posed by regional fragmentation, can likewise moderate multipolar tensions with rival countries because it creates room for win-win interactions. Moreover, it can steer intra-European consensus towards issues over which the potential for internal controversy is low. Similarly, delegation is not just a means to overcome internal contestation.

Delegation of responsibilities and leadership to EU institutions facilitates interaction with other multilateral organisations, while lead groups, thanks to their flexibility and speedier decision-making, can more easily initiate, join and sustain multilateralisation or selective engagement actions.

The EU is a powerful diplomatic machine capable of establishing several dialogue platforms and enhancing relations simultaneously at different levels: relations with external actors, across policy sectors and within the Union. It relies on well-oiled mechanisms for collaboration with allied countries and partners, most notably the United States. It also has a structural predisposition to engage with regional institutions, while its multilateral nature generally gives it access to conflict and crisis parties that tend to see it as a more neutral interlocutor. At the same time, the multi-sectoral structure of EUFSP allows for asymmetrical and selective interventions that are different in focus, nature, size and scope, to address different dimensions of conflicts and crises. Its multi-actor character involves that policy can start off from multiple points within the Union (the various EU institutions and member states, alone or in groups) and be sustained over time in spite of internal differences and even contestation.

The relational nature of EUFSP emerges in full from the above picture. In international security matters, the EU's actorness depends on the constraints imposed by the interplay between the contextual factors themselves (the constitutive dependence element of EUFSP's relational nature) and the non-linear processes through which the EU and its member states cope with and mitigate their effects (the institutional resilience element of EUFSP's relational nature). While all international agents are, to an extent, defined by the way they adapt to the context in which their foreign policy unfolds, the multi-actor and multi-sector governance structures presiding over EUFSP lends it a singular character: the EU is better suited to enter multiple engagements with conflict actors than most states and more resourceful than most international organisation in substantiating those engagements. The features that define its way of doing business in crisis management reflect this character.

The modes of handling multipolar pressures in the crises examined in this chapter reveal that the EU's action in international security is still more multilateralist (rule-oriented) than geopolitical (power-driven): the EU is better apt to build inclusive coalitions within or in support of international regimes than to engage in power contests. The EU has raised its 'geopolitical' actorness, but this remains anchored in, and limited by, a Euro-Atlantic order whose centre of gravity lies in Washington. The modes of managing regional fragmentation paint a picture of an elastic and pragmatist EU that selects and deploys tactically a number of instruments for actions that are often far removed from the ideal of a normative power. Finally, the cacophony of voices characterising the foreign and security policy debates within the Union overwhelms, but cannot silence altogether, the deeper polyphonic harmonies that allow EU member states to overcome their divisions, including through delegation, thereby constituting a polymorphic and collective actor.

Multilateralist and Atlanticist, elastic and pragmatist, polymorphic and collective: the EU's relational power is encapsulated in these elements. While these features have shown a significant degree of stability over time, they have not remained static, constantly adapting to a changing context. Transformation has happened in the past and will happen again. In the next chapter, which concludes our inquiry, we imagine how EU actorness can change in the near future.

Notes

1 Council of the EU, *A Strategic Compass for Security and Defence*, 14 March 2022, p. 13, https://www.eeas.europa.eu/node/410976_en, p. 7.

2 Philip de Man, Gustavo Müller and Andriy Tyushka, "Proposals to Improve the EU's Engagement in Conflict Resolution, Prevention and Mediation", in *ENGAGE Working Papers*, No. 14, November 2022, https://www.engage-eu.eu/publications/the-eus-engagement-in-conflict-resolution-prevention-and-mediation.

3 Philipp Genschel, Lauren Leek and Jordy Weyns, "War and Integration. The Russian Attack on Ukraine and the Institutional Development of the EU", *Journal of European Integration*, Vol. 45, No. 3, 2023, pp. 345–360 at p. 344, https://doi.org/10.1080/07036337.2023.2183397.

4 Oriol Costa and Esther Barbé, "A Moving Target. EU Actorness and the Russian Invasion of Ukraine", *Journal of European Integration*, Vol. 45, No. 3, 2023, pp. 431–446 at p. 431, https://doi.org/10.1080/07036337.2023.2183394.

5 Christopher Hill, "The Capability-Expectations Gap: Or Conceptualising Europe's International Role", *Journal of Common Market Studies*, Vol. 31, No. 3, September 1993, pp. 305–328, https://doi.org/10.1111/j.1468-5965.1993.tb00466.

6 It is worth noticing that a negative record in crisis and conflict management is not exclusive to the EU. The United States and other powers, as well as the United Nations and regional security-focussed organisations have often

proved unable to create the conditions for sustainable peace. Again, this is, in part, a consequence of the complex local dynamics and fragmentation of regions, as well as the growing competition among global and regional powers which, in a self-reinforcing vicious cycle, create constant disincentives to collaborate. Clearly, it is not just EU foreign and security policy that is constrained by these systemic factors. See, for example, Richard N. Haass, "The Age of Nonpolarity", *Foreign Affairs*, Vol. 87, No. 3, May/June 2008, pp. 44–56; Charles A. Kupchan, *No One's World. The West, the Rising Rest, and the Coming Global Turn*, Oxford/New York, Oxford University Press, 2012; Cedric De Coning and Mateja Peter, *United Nations Peace Operations in a Changing Global Order*, Cham, Palgrave Macmillan, 2019, https://doi.org/10.1007/978-3-319-99106-1.

7 Riccardo Alcaro and Hylke Dijkstra, "Re-imagining EU Foreign and Security Policy in a Complex and Contested World", *The International Spectator*, Vol. 59, No. 1, 2024, pp. 1–18, https://doi.org/10.1080/03932729.2024.2304028; Sarah van Bentum and Gregor Walter-Drop, "Unlocking EU Foreign and Security Potential: Measures to Mitigate Internal Contestation, Regional Fragmentation and Multipolar Competition", in *JOINT Research Papers*, No. 24, February 2024, https://www.jointproject.eu/?p=1954.

8 Riccardo Alcaro et al., "A Joined-Up Union, a Stronger Europe. A Conceptual Framework to Investigate EU Foreign and Security Policy in a Complex and Contested World", in *JOINT Research Papers*, No. 8, March 2022, https://www.jointproject.eu/?p=969, see in particular Section 2.

9 Alcaro and Dijkstra group these measures under the broader heading of "coalitional mitigation measures". See Riccardo Alcaro and Hylke Dijkstra, "Re-imagining EU Foreign and Security Policy in a Complex and Contested World", *The International Spectator*, Vol. 59, No. 1, March 2024, pp. 1–18, https://doi.org/10.1080/03932729.2024.2304028, p. 9.

10 "Functional mitigation measures", according to Alcaro and Dijkstra, who also add issue-linkages. See Riccardo Alcaro and Hylke Dijkstra, "Re-imagining EU Foreign and Security Policy in a Complex and Contested World", *The International Spectator*, Vol. 59, No. 1, March 2024, pp. 1–18, https://doi.org/10.1080/03932729.2024.2304028, p. 9.

11 "Institutional delegation measures", according to Alcaro and Dijkstra's categorisation. See Riccardo Alcaro and Hylke Dijkstra, "Re-imagining EU Foreign and Security Policy in a Complex and Contested World", *The International Spectator*, Vol. 59, No. 1, March 2024, pp. 1–18, https://doi.org/10.1080/03932729.2024.2304028, p. 8.

12 Obviously, the EU's performance in handling the contextual challenges varies from case to case and even in the same case it changes over the years. For a review of different cases, see Riccardo Alcaro and Hylke Dijkstra (eds), "Re-imagining EU Foreign and Security Policy in a Complex and Contested World", Special Issue: *The International Spectator*, Vol. 59, No. 1, 2024, https://www.tandfonline.com/toc/rspe20/59/1.

13 Sven Biscop, "No Peace from Corona: Defining EU Strategy for the 2020s", *Journal of European Integration*, Vol. 42, No. 8, 2020, pp. 1009–1023; Jolyon Howorth, "The EU's Chair Was Missing at the Ukraine Table",

European View, Vol. 21, No. 1, pp. 27–35, 2022, https://journals.sagepub.com/doi/full/10.1177/17816858221089371.

14 Zachary Paikin, "Great Power Rivalry and the Weakening of Collective Hegemony: Revisiting the Relationship between International Society and International Order", *Cambridge Review of International Affairs*, Vol. 34, No. 1, 2021, pp. 22–45, https://doi.org/10.1080/09557571.2020.1720602.

15 Riccardo Alcaro, "Weathering the Geopolitical Storms: The Ever-elusive Success of EU Policy towards Iran", *The International Spectator*, Vol. 59, No. 1, 2024, pp. 98–119, https://doi.org/10.1080/03932729.2023.2273852.

16 Christer Ahlström, "The EU Strategy against Proliferation of Weapons of Mass Destruction", in Shannon N. Kile (ed.), *Europe and Iran. Perspectives on Non-proliferation*, Oxford, Oxford University Press, 2005, pp. 27–46, https://www.sipri.org/node/1633; Riccardo Alcaro, *Europe and Iran's Nuclear Crisis. Lead Groups and EU Foreign Policymaking*, Cham, Palgrave Macmillan, 2018, see in particular Chapter 5.

17 Tarja Cronberg, "No EU, No Iran Deal: The EU's Choice between Multilateralism and the Transatlantic Link", *The Nonproliferation Review*, Vol. 24, No. 3–4, 2017, pp. 243–259, https://doi.org/10.1080/10736700.2018.1432321.

18 Riccardo Alcaro, *Europe and Iran's Nuclear Crisis. Lead Groups and EU Foreign Policymaking*, Cham, Palgrave Macmillan, 2018, see in particular Chapter 9.

19 Riccardo Alcaro, "Europe's Defence of the Iran Nuclear Deal: Less than a Success, More than a Failure", in *The International Spectator*, Vol. 56, No. 1, 2021, pp. 55–72, https://doi.org/10.1080/03932729.2021.1876861.

20 Sebastian Harnisch, "Minilateral Cooperation and Transatlantic Coalition-Building", *European Security*, Vol. 16, No. 1, 2007, pp. 1–27, https://doi.org/10.1080/09662830701442261.

21 Julien Barnes-Dacey and Daniel Levy, "Making the Most of Geneva II", in *ECFR Commentaries*, 17 January 2014, https://ecfr.eu/?p=5377.

22 Council of the EU, *Terms of Reference of an International Contact Group on Venezuela*, 30 January 2019, https://www.consilium.europa.eu/media/38043/st05958-en19-icg-terms-of-reference.pdf.

23 Anna Ayuso et al., "Constraints, Dilemmas and Challenges for EU Foreign Policy in Venezuela", *The International Spectator*, Vol. 59, No. 1, 2024, pp. 140–160, https://doi.org/10.1080/03932729.2023.2289647.

24 Tarja Cronberg, "No EU, No Iran Deal: The EU's Choice between Multilateralism and the Transatlantic Link", *The Nonproliferation Review*, Vol. 24, No. 3–4, 2017, pp. 243–259, https://doi.org/10.1080/10736700.2018.1432321; Riccardo Alcaro, *Europe and Iran's Nuclear Crisis. Lead Groups and EU Foreign Policymaking*, Cham, Palgrave Macmillan, 2018, see in particular Chapter 8.

25 Riccardo Alcaro, "Weathering the Geopolitical Storms: The Ever-elusive Success of EU Policy towards Iran", *The International Spectator*, Vol. 59, No. 1, 2024, pp. 98–119, https://doi.org/10.1080/03932729.2023.2273852.

26 Giulio Pugliese, "The European Union's Security Intervention in the Indo-Pacific: Between Multilateralism and Mercantile Interests", *Journal of Intervention and Statebuilding*, Vol. 17, No. 1, 2023, pp. 76–98,

https://doi.org/10.1080/17502977.2022.2118425. See also, Luis Simón, Daniel Fiott and Octavian Manea, *Two Fronts, One Goal. Euro-Atlantic Security in the Indo-Pacific Age*, The Marathon Initiative, August 2023, https://themarathoninitiative.org/wp-content/uploads/2023/08/Two-Fronts-One-Goal-website-publication-v.2.pdf; Zachary Paikin, "Great Power Rivalry and the Weakening of Collective Hegemony: Revisiting the Relationship between International Society and International Order", *Cambridge Review of International Affairs*, Vol. 34, No. 1, 2021, pp. 22–45, https://doi.org/10.1080/09557571.2020.1720602; Zachary Paikin et al., "The Rise of Mega-Regions Eurasia, the Indo-Pacific, and the Transatlantic Alliance in a Reshaped World Order", in *CEPS In-depth Analysis*, November 2022, https://www.ceps.eu/?p=38396.

27 Steven Blockmans, "The Birth of a Geopolitical EU", *European Foreign Affairs Review*, Vol. 27, No. 2, August 2022, pp. 155–160, https://doi.org/10.54648/eerr2022016. See also, Nathalie Tocci, "The Paradox of Europe's Defense Moment", *Texas National Security* Review, Vol. 6, No. 1, 2022–2023, pp. 99–108, https://doi.org/10.26153/tsw/44441; Max Bergman and Sophia Besch, "Why European Defense Still Depends on America", in *Foreign Affairs*, 7 March 2023, https://www.foreignaffairs.com/node/1130056; Kristi Raik, Steven Blockmans, Anna Osypchuk and Anton Suslov, "EU Policy towards Ukraine: Entering Geopolitical Competition over European Order", *The International Spectator*, Vol. 59, No. 1, 2024, pp. 39–58, https://doi.org/10.1080/03932729.2023.2296576.

28 Catherine Wolfram, Simon Johnson and Łukasz Rachel, "The Price Cap on Russian Oil Exports, Explained", in *Belfer Center Policy Briefs*, December 2022, https://www.hks.harvard.edu/node/310743. See also, Michael Emerson and Steven Blockman, The $300 Billion Question – How to get Russia to Pay for Ukraine's Reconstruction, in *SCEEUS Guest Platform for Eastern Europe Policy*, No. 4, 14 December 2022, https://www.ceps.eu/?p=38555; Mitchell A. Orenstein, "The European Union's Transformation after Russia's Attack on Ukraine", *Journal of European Integration*, Vol. 45, No. 3, 2023, pp. 333–342, https://doi.org/10.1080/07036337.2023.2183393; Max Bergman, "Europe Needs a Paradigm Shift in How It Supports Ukraine", in *CSIS Commentaries*, 17 January 2024, https://www.csis.org/node/108942.

29 Gëzim Vizoka and John Doyle, "Neo-Functional Peace: The European Union Way of Resolving Conflicts", *Journal of Common Market Studies*, Vol. 54, No. 4, 2016, pp. 862–867, https://doi.org/10.1111/jcms.12342.

30 Sarah van Bentum and Gregor Walter-Drop, "Unlocking EU Foreign and Security Potential: Measures to Mitigate Internal Contestation, Regional Fragmentation and Multipolar Competition", in *JOINT Research Papers*, No. 24, February 2024, https://www.jointproject.eu/?p=1954.

31 Elena Baracani, "Evaluating EU Actorness as a State-Builder in 'Contested' Kosovo", *Geopolitics*, Vol. 25, No. 2, 2020, pp. 362–386, https://doi.org/10.1080/14650045.2018.1563890.

32 Anna-Sophie Maass, "The Actorness of the EU's State-Building in Ukraine – Before and after Crimea", *Geopolitics*, Vol. 25, No. 2, 2020, pp. 387–406, https://doi.org/10.1080/14650045.2018.1559149.

33 Andrew Lohsen and Pierre Morcos, "Understanding the Normandy Format and Its Relation to the Current Standoff with Russia", in *CSIS Critical Questions*, 9 February 2022, https://www.csis.org/node/63952; Kristi Raik, Steven Blockmans, Anna Osypchuk and Anton Suslov, "EU Policy towards Ukraine: Entering Geopolitical Competition over European Order", *The International Spectator*, Vol. 59, No. 1, March 2024, pp. 39–58, https://doi.org/10.1080/03932729.2023.2296576. According to Sten Rynning, the failure of the Normandy framework was all but certain due to the misguided assumption of a 'concert of Europe' on which the exercise was based (Sten Rynning, "The False Promise of Continental Concert: Russia, the West and the Necessary Balance of Power", *International Affairs*, Vol. 91, No. 3, 2015, pp. 539–552).

34 Jorge Guzmán and Mónica Rico Benitez, "A New Role for the EU in Venezuela", in *CEPS Expert Opinions*, 4 December 2020, https://www.ceps.eu/?p=31515.

35 Rosa Jiménez, "Borrell: la misión de observación electoral de la UE hizo avanzar la democracia venezolana", in *EuroEFE Euroactiv*, 26 January 2022, https://euroefe.euractiv.es/?p=55141.

36 Anna Ayuso et al., "Constraints, Dilemmas and Challenges for EU Foreign Policy in Venezuela", *The International Spectator*, Vol. 59, No. 1, 2024, pp. 140–160, https://doi.org/10.1080/03932729.2023.2289647.

37 Cornelius Adebahr, *Europe and Iran. The Nuclear Deal and Beyond*, London/New York, Routledge, 2017; Riccardo Alcaro, "Weathering the Geopolitical Storms: The Ever-elusive Success of EU Policy towards Iran", *The International Spectator*, Vol. 59, No. 1, 2024, pp. 98–119, https://doi.org/10.1080/03932729.2023.2273852.

38 Dimitris Bouris, *The European Union and Occupied Palestinian Territories. State Building without a State*, London/New York, Routledge, 2014.

39 Sinem Akgül-Açıkmeşe and Soli Özel, "EU Policy towards the Israel-Palestine Conflict: The Limitations of Mitigation Strategies", *The International Spectator*, Vol. 59, No. 1, March 2024, pp. 59–78, https://doi.org/10.1080/03932729.2024.2309664.

40 Aron Lund, "Helping Syria without Helping Assad: A Zero-sum Game for Brussels?", in Francesco Salesio Schiavi (ed.), "Aid and Diplomacy: The EU Donors' Conference for Syria and Türkiye", in *MED This Week*, 24 March 2023, https://www.ispionline.it/en?p=122328; Caterina Bedin, Tiffany Guendouz and Agnès Levallois, "From Conflict Management to Shielding EU Stability: How Syria's Fragmentation Diverted the EU(FSP) from Action to Reaction", *The International Spectator*, Vol. 59, No. 1, 2024, pp. 79–97, https://doi.org/10.1080/03932729.2023.2277212.

41 There is a case to be made for the prioritisation and compartmentalisation of the Iranian nuclear dispute, the wisdom of which was retroactively proved by the failure of the Trump administration's alternative strategy of maximum pressure, which explicitly linked the nuclear and regional issues together. Still, the notion that the resolution of the nuclear issue could have a stabilising effect on regional divisions in the long term remain an hypothetical, albeit a reasonable one.

42 Eugenia da Conceição-Heldt and Sophie Meunier, "Speaking with a Single Voice: Internal Cohesiveness and External Effectiveness of the EU in Global Governance", *Journal of European Public Policy*, Vol. 21, No. 7, 2014, pp. 961–979, https://doi.org/10.1080/13501763.2014.913219.

43 Pernille Rieker and Mathilde Tomine Eriksdatter Giske, "Conceptualising the Multi-Actor Character of EU(rope)'s Foreign Policy", in *JOINT Research Papers*, No. 2, October 2021, https://www.jointproject.eu/?p=538; Marco Siddi, Tyyne Karjalainen and Juha Jukela, "Differentiated Cooperation in the EU's Foreign and Security Policy: Effectiveness, Accountability, Legitimacy", *The International Spectator*, Vol. 57, No. 1, March 2022, pp. 107–123, https://doi.org/10.1080/03932729.2022.2026683; Maria Giulia Amadio Viceré and Monika Sus, "Differentiated Cooperation as the Mode of Governance in EU Foreign Policy", *Contemporary Security Policy*, Vol. 44, No. 1, 2023, pp. 4–34, https://doi.org/10.1080/13523260.2023.2168854; Pernille Rieker and Mathilde Tomine Eriksdatter Giske, *European Actorness in a Shifting Geopolitical Order. European Strategic Autonomy Through Differentiated Integration*, Cham, Palgrave Macmillan, 2024, https://doi.org/10.1007/978-3-031-44546-0.

44 Riccardo Alcaro and Hylke Dijkstra, "Re-imagining EU Foreign and Security Policy in a Complex and Contested World", *The International Spectator*, Vol. 59, No. 1, 2024, pp. 1–18, https://doi.org/10.1080/03932729.2024.2304028.

45 Pol Bargués, Assem Dandashly, Hylke Dijkstra, Gergana Noutcheva, "Engagement against All Odds? Navigating Member States' Contestation of EU Policy on Kosovo", *The International Spectator*, Vol. 59, No. 1, 2024, pp. 19–38, https://doi.org/10.1080/03932729.2023.2295893.

46 Anna Ayuso et al., "Constraints, Dilemmas and Challenges for EU Foreign Policy in Venezuela", *The International Spectator*, Vol. 59, No. 1, 2024, pp. 140–160, https://doi.org/10.1080/03932729.2023.2289647.

47 Raffaella A. Del Sarto, "Stuck in the Logic of Oslo: Europe and the Israeli-Palestinian Conflict", *The Middle East Journal*, Vol. 73, No. 3, 2019, pp. 376–396, https://doi.org/10.3751/73.3.12; Sinem Akgül-Açıkmeşe and Soli Özel, "EU Policy towards the Israel-Palestine Conflict: The Limitations of Mitigation Strategies", *The International Spectator*, Vol. 59, No. 1, 2024, pp. 59–78, https://doi.org/10.1080/03932729.2024.2309664.

48 Riccardo Alcaro and Marco Siddi, "Lead Groups in EU Foreign Policy: The Cases of Iran and Ukraine", *European Review of International Studies*, Vol. 8, No. 2, 2021, pp. 143–165, https://doi.org/10.1163/21967415-08020016.

49 Christoph Schwegmann, "The Contact Group and Its Impact on the European Institutional Structure", in *EUISS Occasional Papers*, No. 16, June 2000, https://www.iss.europa.eu/node/103.

50 International Commission on the Balkans, *The Balkans in Europe's Future*, Sofia: Bosch Stiftung, King Badouin Foundation, German Marshall Fund of the United States, Stewart Mott Foundation, 2005.

51 Riccardo Alcaro, *Europe and Iran's Nuclear Crisis. Lead Groups and EU Foreign Policy-Making*, Cham, Palgrave Macmillan, 2018, see in particular Chapter 7; Aniseh Bassiri Tabrizi and Benjamin Kienzle, "The High

Representative and *Directoires* in European Foreign Policy: The Case of the Nuclear Negotiations with Iran", *European Security*, Vol. 29, No. 3, 2020, pp. 320–336, https://doi.org/10.1080/09662839.2020.1798407.

52 Riccardo Alcaro, "Weathering the Geopolitical Storms: The Ever-elusive Success of EU Policy towards Iran", *The International Spectator*, Vol. 59, No. 1, 2024, pp. 98–119, https://doi.org/10.1080/03932729.2023.2273852.

53 Michal Natorski and Karolina Pomorska, "Trust and Decision-making in Times of Crisis: The EU's Response to the Events in Ukraine", *Journal of Common Market Studies*, Vol. 55, No. 1, 2017, pp. 54–70, https://doi.org/10.1111/jcms.12445. See also, Riccardo Alcaro and Marco Siddi, "Lead Groups in EU Foreign Policy: The Cases of Iran and Ukraine", *European Review of International Studies*, Vol. 8, No. 2, 2021, pp. 143–165, https://doi.org/10.1163/21967415-08020016.

5 The future(s) of relational power Europe

Throughout this work, we have looked at EU and member states' action in crises and conflicts through a double lens: an outside-in perspective, in which we have observed how multipolar competition, regional fragmentation and internal contestation constrain foreign policy (in Chapter 3), and an inside-out perspective, in which the focus has been on the EU's resilience to these contextual factors (in Chapter 4). In other words, we have traced EUFSP to the interactions between its structures and the specific challenges emanating from the contextual factors, concluding that 'relational power Europe' is multilateralist and Atlanticist, elastic and pragmatist, polymorphic and collective.

During the timeframe under consideration – from the mid-2000s to the early 2020s – the structures presiding over EU foreign and security policy remained largely steady. To be sure, the EU did not stop adjusting after the Lisbon Treaty entered into force in 2009, with novelties introduced into the areas of defence, enlargement and economic statecraft, amongst others. But no change made after the late 2000s altered the balance between EU institutions and member states to the point of re-shaping the structures through which the EU handled the contextual challenges. Still, change to EUFSP structures may well happen in the future – in fact, it is likely to. Demands for reform (even radical reform) have grown louder while, at the same time, political forces advocating for less Europe have become stronger.

The combination of the perceived need for change and the uncertainty about the direction such change may take raises the question of whether the concept of relational power Europe would hold in the presence of modified EUFSP structures. Would our understanding of EU foreign and security policy as constitutively relational – because of its dependence on context and the way it shows resilience to it – still capture how the EU would deal with crises and conflicts? Or would the

DOI: 10.4324/9781003559467-6

EU's modes to handle the contextual challenges change to the point of altering the features of EUFSP, namely its multilateralist, Atlanticist, elastic, pragmatist, polymorphic and collective character?

To answer these questions, in this chapter we project the EU's relational power and its features into the future. We formulate three scenarios encompassing the interaction between the evolution of contextual factors and various options of change of EUFSP governance structures.[1] In a first scenario, EU member state governments embark on an institutional overhaul; low internal contestation is greatly facilitated by growing multipolar competition and worsening regional fragmentation ('reform' scenario); in the second, they opt for sectorial adjustments on the margins, which are facilitated by manageable levels of multipolar competition and internal contestation together with high levels of regional fragmentation ('adjustment' scenario); in the third, they hollow out EUFSP structures due to high internal contestation and an intensification of multipolar competition; this contrasts with the lessening of regional fragmentation ('fracture' scenario). The scenarios are imagined on a mid-term horizon (so around the mid-2030s). Our goal is to explore how a changed EU would handle the contextual factors in each of the three different futures, and to infer from that the features defining the EU's relational power. We conclude that relational power Europe will be attenuated in the first scenario, continues as it is today in the second and all but collapses in the third. In these terms, our focus is on imagining the EU's futural capacity for actorness in international security or, more accurately, its possible transformation, which is crucial for nurturing policy thinking on EUFSP.

The chapter breaks down into five sections. In the first one, we discuss the pressures for changes to EU foreign and security policy that have arisen from various quarters in recent years and contrast it with public opinion trends, so as to get a broad sense of the conditions under which reform or fracture could materialise. The next three sections follow the same two-part structure: they illustrate a particular scenario of evolution of EUFSP governance before discussing how the EU's relational power would present itself in the given scenario. A concluding section summarises the chapter and lays the groundwork for final reflections on Relational Power Europe.

An open future for EU foreign and security policy

In a recent study on public opinion in six EU countries – namely France, Germany, Greece, Italy, Poland and Spain – interviewees were asked to express support for a common European army. Different groups of respondents received different bits of information, ranging from the position of political parties to the identity of politicians in favour or against the proposition. The purpose was to identify which driver had the greatest effect in shaping the respondents' opinion. Contrary to expectations, Europeans (at least in the six countries where the experiment was conducted) were much likelier to trace their support for more EUFSP integration to substantive arguments about the pros and cons of it (even on a radical, indeed unrealistic, proposal such as a common army) than to ideology or party affiliation.[2] Hence, it can be reasonably inferred that there is political room for championing a positive integration agenda, as much as for advocating for contrary options. This 'blank' space can be filled by political entrepreneurs capable of taking the initiative, who can read global affairs in light of the trends in multipolar competition and regional fragmentation and communicate a compelling vision for an EU which is better equipped to face such global challenges.

Calls for reform have indeed intensified in recent years. As discussed in Chapter 1, the inner drive towards greater foreign, security and defence integration kept moving for most of the 1990s and 2000s. Even as the appetite for treaty changes diminished and then dissipated after the Lisbon Treaty entered into force in 2009, internal demand for more EUFSP never abated.

Most importantly from our perspective, from the mid-2010s onwards, such inner drive has combined with outside crises and conflicts to spur many in government, academia and elsewhere to call for a boost of EUFSP structures, especially in defence. US President Trump's open hostility towards the EU has woken up Europeans to the fact that the long-debated US disengagement from Europe is no longer an academic hypothesis but an actual possibility, and that the EU had best step up efforts to take care of its own security.[3] Russia's war of conquest in Ukraine has reinforced the message: it has laid bare structural shortcomings in the EU and member states' ability to sustain strategic competition with a rival power (see Chapter 3) that can best be addressed through greater policy coordination or even institutional integration. A direct consequence of Russia's invasion of Ukraine, namely the EU's renewed commitment to enlargement, including to Ukraine itself, has made the proposition of reform hardly avoidable. Few believe that an enlarged EU can function in its current institutional shape given so many international strains,[4] as recognised by the European Council itself.[5]

The demand for more EUFSP integration has been conveyed through various channels, ranging from academic articles and policy papers to political parties' platforms[6] and innovative processes involving ordinary citizens, such as the 2021–2022 Conference on the Future of Europe.[7] Some EU governments have officially embraced the plan. In January 2023, the French and German foreign ministers mandated a group of experts to provide recommendations for reform,[8] and in May 2023 launched a Group of Friends on Qualified Majority Voting (QMV) in CFSP along with their counterparts from Belgium, Finland, Italy, Luxembourg, the Netherlands, Slovenia and Spain.[9] Shortly thereafter, Enrico Letta and Mario Draghi, two former Italian prime ministers acting upon invitation of the European Council and the Commission, respectively, recommended the strengthening of EU defence policy and economic statecraft as integral to broader efforts aimed at improving the single market and EU competitiveness.[10] These initiatives echo a widespread desire for a stronger EU foreign and security policy that a large section of the European public, with no major differences amongst member states, has consistently expressed for years.[11] Crises such as Brexit, the Covid-19 or the war in Ukraine have not dented the public's preference for common European action in international security; if anything, they have consolidated it.[12]

However, there are forces that resist change. It would be wrong to assume that a more contested world is invariably leading to further EU integration or that the domestic political environment in the EU is uniformly conducive to the reform of EUFSP structures. There are, in fact, numerous and deeply rooted internal obstacles and resistances to reform, also in reaction to great power rivalry and regional fragmentation. The enthusiasm for QMV in CFSP shown by the aforementioned Group of Friends may cool or dissipate after a change in government in any of the group's participants. Besides, their passion is not at all shared by other member state governments, often irrespective of political colour. For instance, a coalition of Nordic and Central-Eastern member states (plus Malta) felt compelled to react to the final report of the Conference on the Future of Europe with a public statement in which they ruled out any treaty change.[13] And the Draghi and Letta reports may well end up being largely ignored, as it happened to previous similar exercises.

Governments are generally reluctant to give up competences, especially when it concerns such sacred paraphernalia of state sovereignty as foreign and defence policy. Particularly in times of growing multipolar competition and regional fragmentation, which are times of instability and uncertainty, public opinion is more supportive of this stance than polls recording enthusiasm for more integration attest. Experts have long observed how public backing of a common foreign, security and defence policy may be large but is also both ignorant and shallow.[14]

Public opinion is ignorant in the sense that citizens become decidedly more tepid once they get acquainted with the trade-offs in terms of sovereignty losses that an integrated CFSP would imply.[15] In addition, support for more EUFSP coexists with support for other, not always compatible, propositions.[16] For instance, the public's eagerness to see a more autonomous EU in a world of rivalry and competition is tempered by a reluctance to see NATO's role in Europe diminished.[17] Public support is shallow because the share of the population willing to make reform of EUFSP structures politically salient is much smaller than the one expressing broad support for it.[18] This shallowness of overall support for a more integrated EUFSP contrasts with the deeper aversion to it cultivated by a smaller but vocal segment of the population. Political parties that for ideological conviction or electoral convenience (or both) are eager to politicise European integration, including in the foreign and security policy field, may thus count on a substantial pool of voters prone to be mobilised.[19] This combination of resistance of governments to yield sovereignty, ignorant and shallow public support for more EUFSP as well as the risks of political instrumentalisation explains the lack of appetite for treaty changes and the relatively slow progress of lesser forms of policy coordination and integration that have characterised the post-Lisbon EU.

In conclusion, while the deterioration of multipolar interactions and the fragmentation of the EU's neighbourhood have given a boost to voices in favour of more integration, endemically higher level of internal contestation of EU politics compared to the 1991–2007 period have prevented any significant step forward. In the mid-2020s, the picture is mixed. Due to renewed inner demand and strong outer pressure, the prospects for reforming EUFSP structures are arguably higher than they have been for the previous 15 years. At the same time, none of the factors that have hindered the institutional development of European foreign and security policy during this period have disappeared. Still, the co-existence of these contrasting forces does not mean that stasis is the only possible outcome of the clash between them. Different scenarios open up.

***

Before delving into the illustration of such scenarios and envisioning how the EU's relational power would look like in each of them, it is worth mentioning the criteria we have followed in building them.

First, we have not engaged in forecasting. Predicting or establishing the chances for each scenario to materialise falls outside our research focus. However, we have paid attention to building scenarios that reflect the empirical evidence that we have reviewed in this section, whereby we have excluded the most radical options and tried to make the scenarios plausible evolutions of existing trends. Second, we have considered multiple dimensions of (dis)integration, including decision-making rules, institutional engineering, ambition and range of common policies, as well as the size of EU resources. Third and finally, we have assumed change happening in multiple policy areas – so not only CFSP and CSDP, but also other ones that have an external dimension, privileging all those policy fields that shape the crisis and conflict management capacity of the EU and its member states.

The scenarios described in the next sections follow the same pattern: initially, we speculate about a particular configuration of the contextual factors that has facilitated changes in the EUFSP structures; we then consider decision-making rules, institutional transformations and the ambition and scope of EUFSP-related common policies. Evidently, in the future the contextual factors may evolve differently and impact the EU differently: the Union may advance or regress at a different pace or even in a different direction in these various dimensions. This implies that our scenarios are somewhat ideal-typical. Their purpose is not to predict the future, but to offer distinguishable frames of reference for the construction of a transformed EU actorness in international security while also providing inputs for policy reflection and discussion.[20]

A resilient Europe in a competitive world

In a first scenario, by the mid-2030s the EU has undergone a significant upgrade of EUFSP structures, mostly driven by a pronounced increase in multipolar competition. Russia has continued to show aggressiveness in Europe and pursue hostile policies in North Africa and the Sahel. The Sino-American competition has escalated to the extent that the United States has moved most of its military resources and diplomatic attention towards the Indo-Pacific. However, it remains committed to NATO and European security as a pillar of its grand strategy to keep hostile powers at bay and re-invest in rules-based regimes. Increased multipolar competition has inflamed further regional tensions and left the European neighbourhood rife with conflict, insecurity, governance breakdown and areas of limited statehood. However, the combination of fiercer geopolitical competition and persistently fragmented regions has lowered contestation within the EU, not least because Eurosceptic nationalist forces have found an unreceptive partner in Washington. Member states have determined that they can better face the contextual challenges only if they share more resources together, including through sounder collective decision-making.

In this scenario, qualified majority voting has replaced unanimity in most instances in which the Council takes CFSP-related decisions. Individual member states can no longer veto common positions on human rights or the adoption of sanctions. Qualified majorities also decide key aspects of EU defence policy, such as the launch and deployment of CSDP missions (although individual member states may opt out), the use of special funds such as the European Peace Facility, and the activation of a crisis toolbox compelling member states to increase their preparedness to face urgent military production needs.

This scenario is also one of institutional empowerment of the EU. While the basic institutional structure (European Council, Council of Ministers, Commission, Parliament) and the main bodies of the EU remain the same, their internal working methods and cooperation mechanisms are enhanced through sustained institutional engineering. Facing numerous challenges in the neighbouring regions, the European Council's capacity for crisis and conflict management is strengthened through the creation of ad hoc crisis/conflict task forces. The task forces, comprising national diplomats coordinated by the EEAS, produce joint conflict analysis and devise policy options that the HRVP reports to EU heads of state and government, including in single-issue summits if the geopolitical magnitude of the crisis warrants it.

The HRVP is given ultimate responsibility for development cooperation, neighbourhood policy, and humanitarian aid (the relevant commissioners for these policy areas are made subordinate to the HRVP). Most importantly, the HRVP along with the Commission president and a newly established defence commissioner convene in a security and defence troika that advises and receives inputs from the European Council. This troika ensures greater alignment between the EU's foreign and security policy goals and its defence targets and military-related industrial capacity.

The troika benefits from a number of innovations in the EU's defence institutional structures, starting with the aforementioned defence commissioner. The establishment of a separate defence portfolio elevates military industrial matters to the same level of importance of other critical dossiers managed by the Commission (from the common market to climate), centralises policy formulation and lends political and budgetary strength to Commission initiatives in this field. The empowerment of the Commission in defence industry matters is complemented with the formalisation of the meetings of defence ministers. A Defence Council separate from its sister configuration for foreign policy, the Foreign Affairs Council (FAC), contributes to delivering more sustained policy coordination because it reinforces the personal commitment of individual defence ministers. Thereby, the EU has become as important a forum for defence discussions as NATO and intra-EU bilateral dialogues. Similarly, the upgrade of the European Parliament (EP) subcommittee on defence to a fully fledged committee has led to more MEPs gaining direct expertise in, and consequently ownership of, defence-related matters, while also creating more democratic accountability for defence decisions.

Another innovation occurring in this scenario is that the capability development plan prepared by European Defence Agency (EDA) sees full involvement and ownership of member states and becomes the main point of reference for EU defence industrial initiatives and budgets. The EDA's greater responsibilities go hand in hand with an increase in resources allocated by the member states to defence, particularly to intra-European defence projects. The development of projects on advanced and sophisticated weapon systems (land, maritime, air, space and cyber-based) within the framework of the Permanent Structured Cooperation (PESCO), as well as an increase in intra-European projects subsidised by the Commission, are perfectly compatible with this reform scenario. The main channels of funding in this regard, namely the European Defence Fund (EDF) and the European Defence Industry Programme (EDIP), benefit from substantial budgets hovering around eight to ten billion euros for the former and around 70–75 billion for the latter (moreover, a flexibility mechanism allows for substantial increases if circumstances require it). It becomes therefore conceivable that the joint development of military capabilities at the EU level and increased cooperation among member states within the PESCO framework enable

European manufacturers to supply about 75 per cent of the total military equipment purchased by EU member states.

In this scenario, the development of more and better-integrated capabilities has expanded the operational capacity of the EU. A unified EU headquarters for CSDP military missions is capable of simultaneously conducting a major military operation (involving around 10,000 units from multinational joint forces) and a smaller one in non-permissive environments, wherein the EU mission is ready to engage in combat. These operations are in addition to smaller ones involving hundreds of personnel (defence capacity building, security force assistance, security sector reform, border monitoring, etc.).

With the United States focussed mostly on the Indo-Pacific, stronger European defence benefits NATO too. European national armed forces have become more interoperable and integrated, thus rebalancing the Alliance's collective defence and deterrence through the consolidation of a European pillar. In addition, the EU is capable to run both the civilian and military aspects of crisis management as well as the stability operations that have been de-prioritised by NATO in light of the prominent threat from Russia, thus enabling a functional division of labour in Europe and especially the southern neighbourhood.

The innovations to EUFSP structures in the reform scenario extend to other policy areas with an external dimension. The enlargement process has benefitted from QMV on all intermediary steps between the opening and closing of the accession negotiation, in that it has anchored the enlargement process in a more technical, depoliticised procedure controlled by the Commission and reduced the risk that member state governments intervene to complicate the accession of one or another candidate country for internal political reasons at every step in the way. Other facilitations work as incentives for candidate countries to adopt the reforms by providing membership benefits during the process and not just at the end.[21]

Novelties have been introduced also into energy policy, which is made at the EU level as much as climate policy is today. A stronger energy diplomacy is carried out by the Commission and is aligned with the EU's decarbonisation diplomacy. The EU promotes joint infrastructure projects abroad and has developed a toolbox to absorb sudden supply and price shocks, which includes measures for automatic solidarity in case energy disruption affects member states differently.

The EU has also significantly strengthened its economic statecraft tools. It has added to the existing set of measures (spanning rules on foreign procurements and subsidies as well as retaliatory actions against politically motivated trade limitations) three critical innovations: the inbound investment screening framework has been upgraded into a single EU standard; alongside it, a unified outbound investment screening tool has been adopted; and finally, the EU has centralised the supervision of member states' enforcement of export controls and other restrictions. These measures have provided greater coherence to the EU's sanction and derisking policies, as they have reduced the scope for national exemptions and deviations from common EU positions.

Finally, this reform scenario would not be possible if the Union did not rely on significantly bigger resources than is the case presently. The EU's budget is assumed to have grown considerably, at least doubling in size, resulting in increased allocations to EUFSP-relevant policies. The budget increase derives from growth in member state contributions, an expansion of EU own resources and the use of common debt instruments modelled on the Next Generation EU post-Covid recovery fund. Besides the energy and digital targets set by the latter, these new facilities provide support for developing specific defence assets, CSDP missions and assistance to Ukraine's reconstruction and, more broadly, the enlargement process.

While this reformed EU is far from being able to execute a unified foreign and security policy akin to that of a sovereign state, it has equipped itself with more resources, greater military production and capabilities, an institutional organisation oriented towards synergy, more efficient systems for protecting against the risk that external powers exploit its internal weaknesses. This more integrated institutional setup has made the Union a more resilient power in that it has reduced its constitutive dependence on context.

A reformed EU has become more capable to resist multipolar pressures in the management of crises and conflicts. The innovations in foreign and defence policy have contributed to better informing EU leaders' decisions, thus giving direction and greater consistency to EU initiatives. The introduction of QMV and the rationalisation and upgrade of foreign and defence policymaking, coupled with the greater alignment of a larger defence industrial base with military targets set at the EU level, has expanded the EU's room for autonomous manoeuvre. The Union has the political-military wherewithal to increase and sustain military assistance to third countries like Ukraine as well as to deploy combat-ready operations in non-permissive environments. It has thus acquired a critical asset to endure competition with rival poles in areas of conflict.[22]

Furthermore, a reformed EU can absorb and react to energy shocks faster. This reduces its vulnerability to the weaponisation of energy supplies by third countries. Similarly, standardised inbound and outbound investment screening mechanisms have given EU member states an additional layer of protection against divide-and-rule tactics by foreign powers. At the same time, the reformed EU's clout over conflict parties has increased due to its expanded authority over the adoption of sanctions and other restrictions through QMV, as well as over the monitoring of member states' compliance. These new competences have limited the opportunities for third countries to exploit differences in the legislative and enforcement regimes of individual member states and therefore cannot easily circumvent or evade EU export control regimes and other restrictions. A reformed EU has also indirectly reduced the room for rival powers to spoil the enlargement process because candidate countries can get significant benefits even before accession, whereby they are incentivised to align with EU policies. In sum, EUFSP structures have become less porous to the constraining effect of intensified multipolar competition and regional fragmentation.

In theory, a reformed EU still favours multilateralisation in order to mitigate multipolar constraints. This is because a reformed EU is a more powerful catalyst of intra-continental relations, most notably with the United Kingdom and Turkey, including within such frameworks as the European Political Community (EPC). It is also a more credible interlocutor for extra-European players and a more appealing partner for other international organisations. Its potential for starting or supporting ad hoc multilateral crisis management undertakings has grown accordingly.

In practice, the greater capacity for sustaining geopolitical pressures has given a reformed EU more alternatives to multilateralisation and especially increased the appeal of strategic partnering with like-minded countries. Indeed, a reformed EU can utilise its new assets in its relations with partners to align coordination more closely with its own strategic preferences rather than those of the partners. To a limited extent this also applies to the United States, which is inclined to take European sensitivities into greater account because of the larger contribution to collective defence within NATO enabled by a reformed EU. However, because the defence of Europe remains even in this scenario a prerogative of NATO, the reformed EU continues to operate within a US-led Euro-Atlantic order. It has managed to increase its specific weight and advance its own priorities more forcefully in that order, as well expand its reach outside the Euro-Atlantic perimeter, but in no way has the EU detached itself from it.

The simplified decision-making rules and rationalised policymaking processes have put a reformed EU in a stronger position to confront challenges emanating from regional fragmentation too. The standing crisis/conflict task forces advising the European Council have facilitated greater information exchange amongst member states. The HRVP has built upon such exchanges and the authority to integrate actions from her or his various portfolios, which include neighbourhood, development and humanitarian aid, to present the Council with more coherent sets of policy options. Consequently, trade-offs between conflict resolution goals and other priorities have become less imbalanced, and the EU can present itself to conflict parties as a more homogeneous and reliable interlocutor. When necessary, a reformed EU builds on tactics of decoupling and selective engagement, while having greater leeway to ensure that limited forms of engagement do not hamper higher-level peace and security efforts.

A reformed EU presupposes by definition a greater commitment to European integration – and consequently EUFSP – by all member states. While internal contestation is therefore less of a problem, member states do disagree, even fundamentally, also in this scenario. Their modes to cope with it has changed significantly, however. On paper, qualified majority voting is as powerful an instrument to overcome internal splits as it gets. In practice, member states continue to strive for consensus, especially on matters of security and defence, in order to avoid estranging individual member states and create stronger common ownership of crisis and conflict management enterprises.[23] In this respect, QMV is less a tie-breaker than an amplifier and accelerator of deliberative processes, as contesting states are compelled to engage in negotiation with a view to finding an agreement so as not to be outvoted. Delegation can still be used in cases in which contestation is so stark that the Council prefers not to force decisions through QMV. EU institutions are likelier to be the beneficiaries of delegation than lead groups, as the latter lose much of their purpose in an EUFSP governance system in which EU policymaking is both quicker and more flexible (which is a key added value of lead groups).

In conclusion, in this scenario the dependence on context of EUFSP is attenuated, while its resilience to contextual challenges has increased. The context, both in its systemic and internal dimensions, has a lesser impact on constituting the EU's actorness in international security than currently is the case. The strengthened institutional set-up reduces the need to permanently adapt to events and augments the EU's capacity to shape such events. The EU's power nonetheless remains relational in the sense that it continues to be based on enhanced relations, but the capacity to do so has grown. The attributes that define its actorness shift consequently.

While both multilateralism and Atlanticism remains defining features of a more resilient EU, they are both tempered. The Union has acquired a greater capacity to engage in power competition, whereby multilateralisation has become more a choice than a necessity, so to speak. And even if it continues to partner with the United States and NATO for the defence of Europe and the amplification of its international influence, a reformed EU has managed to reconcile the lingering commitment to the Atlantic Alliance with a greater capacity to act autonomously on crises and conflicts.

A reformed EU is thus capable of managing a partial US disengagement from Europe and the transatlantic relationship at large. It can also offset some of the consequences of a total disengagement, if that is the direction the United States takes. A reformed EU remains a pragmatist actor that engages with crises and conflicts asymmetrically. Although it is better equipped to cope with varying trade-offs between normative and strategic interests as well as domestically salient priorities and conflict management goals than it is today, competitive multipolarity makes coherence and linearity almost impossible.

Finally, while a reformed EU may not be a single international player, it has become a collective power. The changes through which it has gone have created patterns of policy convergence amongst member states that have eventually made it a much more homogeneous actor. Rather than a complementary track, as it is today in many respects (especially for large member states), EUFSP becomes the main framework for engaging in international security for all EU states. The reformed EU is not a great power, but it has acquired assets that make it a 'pole' capable of engaging in (limited) geopolitical competition with other players of equal or larger size.

An adjusted Europe in a fragmented world

A different scenario assumes that by 2035 multipolar competition has somewhat eased. Still, the prospect for an inclusive, rules-based and cooperative global governance remains elusive, and regional fragmentation has solidified or worsened. Crucially for European security, the United States remains committed to European defence – in fact, it has fully re-established its dominance on the continent through NATO, US-EU relations and bilateral arrangements. At the same time, local conflicts in areas of contested statehood continue to cause humanitarian crises while exacerbating existing divisions in the EU's neighbourhood and beyond. This combination of relatively stable multipolar rivalries and deepening regional fragmentation contributes to maintaining internal contestation inside the EU within manageable limits, but it creates no powerful incentive for bold integration advancements. Still, limited improvements to EUFSP structures have been made across the board compared to the early 2020s: decision-making has been enhanced, institutions upgraded and resources increased.

By 2035, decision-making has moderately improved. The Team Europe initiatives model, whereby EU member states and agencies pool together expertise and resources to promote cooperation and development abroad, has been brought to a higher political-strategic level. The European Council has formally endorsed the practice of lead groups (thus giving more political weight to a point already included in the EU Global Strategy). The lead groups do not gain any special authority over the other member states, but they are expected to coordinate with the HRVP and, when necessary, with other relevant members of the Commission. The HRVP and the EEAS ensure information sharing between the group's insiders and outsiders, convey the latter's sensitivities to the former and take care that the proposed course of action is in line with EU interests as defined in pre-existing documents and declarations. The lead group regularly updates – directly or via the HRVP – the other member states in the European Council and the FAC. Individual lead groups may be endorsed in European Council/FAC conclusions but can also be given a formal mandate in line with relevant treaty provisions.[24] This practice is meant to increase the EU's responsiveness and capacity of proactive involvement in situations of crises and conflicts.

As regional fragmentation worsens, neighbourhood policy and development cooperation have been brought under the overall supervision of the HRVP (as was the case also in the previous scenario). In defence, the post for a defence commissioner is created and the Commission's proposal for a European Defence Industrial Readiness Board is accepted. The latter is a body comprising the Commission (including the HRVP), the EDA and member states tasked with providing advice on priorities in the development of military capabilities. While not as extensive as in the reform scenario, the Permanent Structured Cooperation provides the framework for the development of two or three major projects to develop common capabilities, involving the EU's largest defence players (France, Germany, Italy and Spain). The Commission incentivises joint efforts on research and development via the EDF (whose budget is stable at eight billion for seven years) and on production through an EDIP worth approximately four billion a year. Funding for common procurement and ammunition purchase continue at current levels at least. Overall, by 2035 around half of the EU's military needs are satisfied by EU defence companies. Operationally, a permanent HQ for CSDP military missions is established with the capacity to plan and execute one or two minor operations in a non-permissive environment, beside smaller non-combat missions (both military and civilian). EU-NATO cooperation has experienced modest improvement. The armed forces of NATO European members benefit from EU defence initiatives, which also favour more convergence within NATO's European caucus and increase the European contribution to collective defence and deterrence.

On enlargement, the Commission has been given the authority to determine whether the level of compliance with the *acquis* is sufficient for negotiations to be opened (or closed) simultaneously in several chapters. Contrary to the reform scenario, however, there is no access of candidate countries to common funds.

Gradual adjustments and improvements occur in other areas. The energy solidarity toolbox devised to better absorb shocks has been adopted, and greater interconnection through pipelines and electricity grids has been achieved. The EU has also strengthened its economic statecraft capacity by standardising inbound investment screening mechanisms (but no outbound investment screening is adopted) and enhancing oversight of member states' enforcement of export controls and sanctions.

As for resource generation, this scenario assumes an increase in the EU's financial power, although not nearly as big as in the case of the institutional reform seen above. The common budget grows by a few decimal percentage points thanks to greater member states contributions and EU own resources. The EU cannot count on standing mechanisms to borrow from financial markets to sustain a more ambitious EUFSP, although it retains the option of adopting it to face major emergencies like the Covid-induced economic crisis.

This is a scenario of incremental evolution of existing trends and proposals to adjust the EUFSP governance structures, whereby the conceptualisation of the EU as a 'relational power' remains valid in both its meanings: the Union is still context-dependent and yet has also slightly improved its resilience towards the contextual challenges through the enhancement of its capacity to build on internal and external relations. This 'adjusted' EU is equipped to resist multipolar pressures of low intensity, although it is not in the position to sustain alone prolonged competition in areas of conflict and crisis in highly fragmented regions.

An adjusted EU has marginally increased its ability to exert pressure on conflict parties through greater military production capacity (which supports military assistance to partners) and stronger central supervision of member states' implementation of export controls, sanctions and other restrictions. This is not enough to curtail conflict parties' quest for benefits and protection from the EU's rivals, but it does make engagement with the EU more appealing for them (and therefore influences their decision-making). This is particularly the case for candidate countries, which thanks to a simplified accession process are further incentivised to resist spoiling actions of external powers.

While an adjusted EU has made no major progress towards strategic autonomy, it has developed further assets (in defence, economic statecraft and energy) and institutional solutions (routinisation of lead groups, empowerment of the HRVP) that make cooperation with third parties easier for the EU and more appealing for third parties themselves. Therefore, the EU's propensity for handling crises and conflicts through multilateralisation cannot but consolidate and strengthen.

In addition, the qualitative and quantitative improvements to European defence occurring in this scenario makes an adjusted EU a better complement of NATO. An adjusted EU may thus contribute to a marginal rebalancing of the transatlantic relationship, even if its subordinate status within the Euro-Atlantic order is unchanged. Firmly anchored in a European security system guaranteed by NATO, an adjusted EU is the main instrument to organise political and economic relations with the United Kingdom and Turkey, bilaterally and within the framework of the EPC. Such engagements reinforce the ability of the EU to build coalitions focusing on crises and conflicts, although the continuous reliance on the United States makes the EU's coalition-building capacity contingent on transatlantic cooperation or at least on the absence of transatlantic divergence. In other words, an adjusted EU may become unsustainable in case of a US disengagement from the transatlantic relationship – if that happens, the adjusted EU can either evolve towards a reformed EU or descend into a fractured EU.

An adjusted Union in a context of reduced multipolar competition has more options to address the composite challenges emanating from the fragmentation of states and regions than today. The formal endorsement of lead groups by the European Council makes recourse to this practice, which compounds the sustainability and intensity of engagements with like-minded countries inside and outside of Europe, more systematic. Furthermore, the parallel expansion of the HRVP's portfolio to development, cooperation and humanitarian aid, in addition to foreign policy and defence, allows for a more centralised use of EU assets. When lead groups are active and coordinate with the HRVP, the potential for proactive policymaking of the adjusted EU is considerable. However, the contingent nature of lead groups involves that synergies between the action of member states and that of EU institutions continue to be more ad hoc than structural. Besides, the persistence of the unanimity rule in CFSP and CSDP decisions continues to hamper attempts at resolving the multiples dimensions of conflicts. Tensions persist between conflict resolution objectives and other concerns prioritised by member states, as trade-offs inevitably lean towards the latter. Consequently, decoupling and selective engagement with specific issues remain critical strategies to handle regional fragmentation risks.

In this scenario, internal contestation manifests itself in a manner not too dissimilar from how it does presently. While the scenario of an adjusted EU is compatible with generalised support across member states for a rationalisation of Union resources and a partial strengthening of EU institutions, the member states remain the masters of EUFSP. The small changes made to decision-making rules marginally increase the use of deliberation as the principal instrument to address internal divisions. At the same time, the delegation of crisis or conflict management to EU institutions or groups of states to avoid dealing with contentious issues continues to be attractive to member states. In fact, the empowerment of the HRVP and, above all, the European Council's formal endorsement of the practice of lead groups create stronger incentives to make use of them through delegation.

In conclusion, the relational nature of EUFSP consolidates and strengthens in the adjustment scenario. The EU member states have found enough consensus for making the institutional set-up of their foreign and security policy more coherent due to persistent fragmentation dynamics in their neighbourhood. At the same time, the relative manageability of multipolar rivalries opens opportunities for strengthening multilateral governance. Accordingly, the attributes of a relational power Europe acquire a more pronounced character.

This adjusted EU has sharpened its multilateralist identity precisely because it has developed stronger assets to promote and sustain multilateral engagements, but not to sustain high-level autonomous action on crises and conflicts. For the same reason, an adjusted EU is structurally inclined to seek strategic partnering both as a complementary force to multilateralisation and as an alternative to it. Just like today, such strategic partnering means by and large the pursuit of transatlantic convergence and a willingness to follow the United States' lead, although the Europeans are marginally better equipped to have Washington pay heed to their preferences.

An adjusted EU still engages with the multiple contextual challenges asymmetrically and discriminately, based on unavoidable trade-offs between its normative and strategic interests, the domestic priorities of its member states and the structural constraints on EUFSP. Regional fragmentation and the multiplication of risks require elasticity: the institutional and resource rationalisation the EU has gone through in this scenario enables greater synergies between different policy actions. This has strengthened the adaptive and resilient character that informs much of the EU's pragmatist identity today.

Finally, an adjusted EU very much remains a non-homogeneous collective actor, given that its nature as a supranational-intergovernmental hybrid has remained unaltered. CFSP consolidates further as a complement to member states' national policies whenever it contributes to amplifying their international clout. An adjusted EU is also a sharper supplement of national policies on issues on which member states cannot have a leading role, such as enlargement. But EU foreign and security policy remains an articulation of national foreign and security policies (as it is presently the case), not the other way round as in the previous scenario. The adjusted EU is no security power, as it remains a polymorphic actor structurally dependent on transatlantic relations, multilateral engagement and partnerships; still, it has acquired assets to reduce the reactive nature of its foreign and security policy.

A disjointed Europe in a contested world

The third scenario is based on the assumption that a combination of higher multipolar competition and lower levels of fragmentation in the EU's neighbourhood has eroded intra-EU consensus on the strengthening of EUFSP structures. The United States has shifted its focus away from Europe to the Indo-Pacific to confront China, while significantly refraining from engaging in multilateral governance. While the United States has not fully abandoned Europe, it subordinates its relations with individual European countries to the goal of ensuring US primacy over China and Russia – and ultimately Europe itself. Consequently, unlike in the first scenario, the United States' reduced commitment to Europe has not triggered EU integration. On the contrary, it has created a race for improving bilateral relations with the foreign powers that EU countries may want to counterbalance against, appease or bandwagon with. EU countries pursue separate engagements mostly with the United States, but also Turkey, China, Russia itself and others still to minimise the impact of lingering crises and conflicts on their most immediate domestic interests, ranging from energy security to migration control. The neighbouring regions of the EU remain relatively stable, disincentivising EU governments to embark in joined-up actions.

In this scenario, even if the Lisbon Treaty remains in force, the Union functions within a looser institutional framework: decision-making becomes more rigid, governance structures are more disjointed and resource generation loses steam. The coalescing of a number of member states into an anti-QMV front has added more inflexibility to EU foreign policy decision-making. The EU heads of state and government have re-affirmed – through statements, non-papers and eventually Council conclusions – the purely intergovernmental nature of all decisions concerning foreign, security and defence policy. Accordingly, the room for institutional engineering solutions designed to bypass the unanimity constraint has all but disappeared. The practice of lead groups has been openly contested by some member states and the European Council has endorsed language opposing it.

The stiffening of decision-making practices has gone along with the absence of any reform aimed at fostering structural synergies in the college of commissioners. Not only has the Commission's composition remained anchored in the rule of one commissioner per member state, but the portfolios of the commissioners (with the partial exception of the vice-presidents) have retained formal equal status and autonomy from each other. The HRVP has received no additional competences and has remained excluded from Commission's decisions on neighbourhood policies, development cooperation and humanitarian aid.

By 2035, the defence sector has undergone governance fragmentation and a reduction in the development and production of joint military capabilities, as well as a scaling down of the potential deployment of operations. Capability development planning does not benefit from any steering body but remains the responsibility of member states operating in a disjointed manner. The EDA's role becomes more marginal, also as a result of a progressive budget reduction. Permanent Structured Cooperation is only used for small projects by a few states with variable geometry compositions (i.e., no core of the four major actors is created). Joint procurement and ammunition acquisition initiatives have been abandoned. The EDF's allocation has fallen to less than one billion per year, and that of EDIP has not exceeded ten billion to be distributed over seven years. There have been no innovations in terms of planning and conducting military operations; the headquarters have continued to be established on an ad hoc basis according to the framework nation model. In light of all this, the EU is only capable of conducting minor operations in permissive environments. EU-NATO cooperation has shrunk, insofar as the Union provides no significant added value and the United States has largely abdicated from its role as the Alliance's driving force, maintaining just a relatively small force in Europe to keep a degree of deterrence against Russia.

The rules governing the enlargement process have not changed, so member states have retained their right to block the accession process of candidate countries at every step and on the basis of political (as opposed to technical) reasons. Similarly, no package to strengthen resilience to shocks in energy prices and supplies has been adopted, and therefore intra-European solidarity in emergency situations relies solely on the contingent willingness of states to adopt ad hoc measures. There has been no expansion of the EU's economic statecraft tools; in fact, the inbound investment screening framework has not been upgraded, while not all member states have even adopted a screening mechanism. Oversight for the enforcement of export controls and sanctions has remained at the national level.

This scenario of governance fracture is compatible with (or rather a reflection of) a stagnating EU budget and a reduction in the share of it that finances CFSP and related policies. Member states' contributions remain unchanged or even decrease, while the option of raising EU own resources through common borrowing is explicitly prohibited in some member states.

In this scenario, the EU is less apt to take decisions that produce synthesis rather than compromises based on the lowest common denominator. Multipolar competition, and especially the United States' desire to confront China heads-on in the Indo-Pacific, has fractured the EU. Even if the fragmentation of the European neighbourhoods does not worsen, the EU lacks institutional and political solutions that facilitate the operationalisation of common positions and is endowed with fewer and less sophisticated capabilities and modest financial resources. Against this background, the EU's relational power undergoes significant change, as the modes of managing contextual challenges inevitably lose their edge.

A fractured EU is less capable of deflecting the mounting challenges of multipolar pressures. The greater rigidity of the decision-making rules, the further fragmentation along national lines of the defence market and the general reduction of common resources to be allocated to EUFSP shatter any aspiration for autonomy. The inability to provide military assistance to partners and deploy anything bigger than a few hundred-strong CSDP mission makes the EU incapable of sustaining geopolitical competition in conflict theatres. The lack of an automatic solidarity tool to deal with energy price or supply shocks, as well as the weakness and fragmentation of the system for monitoring inbound foreign investments, opens up gaps for external powers to wedge themselves into the decision-making and political processes of the EU.

The EU's ability to put pressure on conflict actors is also structurally weakened because the Union has greater difficulty in adopting restrictive measures (given the persistence and indeed the tightening of the unanimity rule) and because it does not have authority over the enforcement of EU restriction regimes by national authorities. This reduced EU influence over crisis and conflict parties also extends to candidate countries. The latter do not receive any incentive during the accession process to accelerate alignment with EU policies. Furthermore, they are more exposed to the political oscillations of member state governments, each of which retains the authority to hinder the enlargement process to the point of blocking it for political rather than technical reasons.

A fractured EU has greater difficulty in organising relations with countries like the United Kingdom and Turkey, or at least in catalysing the organisation of intra-continental relations upon itself. Formats like the EPC become simple ceremonial settings where people meet but no policy is decided or coordinated. This fractured EU is in a relationship of fundamental subordination to NATO, since it does not contribute even indirectly to collective defence and deterrence, nor does it offer comparative advantages in terms of division of labour.

A fractured EU in a context of rampant multipolar competition and US disengagement from multilateral fora has a lower propensity to use multilateralisation as a tool to manage crises and conflicts. A Union weakened in terms of foreign and security policy may still point to rules-based multilateral regimes as the framework in which conflict management and resolution should be conducted. Yet given the declining capacity of a fractured EU to lead peace processes or initiate multilateral conflict management mechanisms, the use of multilateralisation is invariably set to wane. Consequently, strategic partnerships – mostly, but not only, with the United States – become an obligatory choice for EU countries willing to deflect multipolar pressures on their foreign and security policies.

However, the fractured EU has considerably reduced the specific weight of Europe within the Euro-Atlantic order, which has become structured as a 'hub and spokes' system irradiating from the United States, with the bilateral dimension of EU member states' relations with Washington carrying significant more weight than the multilateral one. A fractured EU is capable of contributing to the defence of Europe only marginally (although individual states may well increase their own share for it), and remains profoundly dependent on the United States in most aspects. It goes without saying that such a Union is not capable of sustaining further US disengagement from Europe.

A fractured EU is also unsuitable for generating an integrated approach to regional fragmentation challenges even if they are lower in intensity than the early 2020s. Several elements contribute to this: the tightening of decision-making rules, the rigid separation of portfolios relevant to foreign and security policy within the Commission, the weakness of coordination mechanisms, as well as the abandonment of the practice of lead groups. Resolving tensions between conflict management objectives and national priorities becomes extremely difficult, given the authority of individual states to assert their preferences. Decoupling, namely the temporary limitation of the EU's interaction with a conflict party to a single issue with the view to expanding the dialogue agenda at a later stage, is no longer appealing because the EU is not equipped to sustain incremental engagements. Selective engagement remains an option for member states who want to use EU tools to ensure at least minimal participation in conflict management. Overall, however, EU cooperation partnerships weaken.

Challenges emanating from internal contestation find few remedies in a fractured EU. Deliberative processes become longer in light of the tightening of decision-making rules, and invariably slide into drawn-out negotiations in which the unanimity rule and the general disregard for alternative options give structural advantages to contesting parties. Delegation to common institutions remains a viable option, although such institutions have fewer assets at their disposal. Similarly, the abandonment of the practice of lead groups limits the capacity to engender a higher level of pro-activeness on the part of the EU. The fractured EU is generally hardly able to go beyond lower common denominator-based positions and ends up far removed from playing a cohesive role in crisis and conflict management. It is at best a technocratic platform serving at the behest of member states who may take initiatives to serve their particular interests.

In conclusion, in this scenario a heavy imbalance weighs on the relational nature of EUFSP. The modes of handling the contextual factors allowed for by a fractured institutional set-up are so weak that the EU's actorness in international security shrinks to the point of almost disappearing. The characteristics that define this actorness therefore undergo a profound change.

A fractured EU has diluted its multilateralist identity because it is less capable of initiating and sustaining inclusive and cooperative crisis management processes. A fractured EU is a collection of individual states that conduct a more 'geopolitically' oriented security policy (in the sense that it is power-driven). There are more initiatives and coping strategies than those occurring in an adjusted EU, and they are led by individual member states. The result is a disjointed Union. Most member states have opted for a position of structural subordination to other great powers, most notably the United States even if other external beneficiaries cannot be ruled out (states like Cyprus or Hungary or Western Balkan candidate countries, for instance, may want to hedge between the United States and China and even Russia).

A fractured EU has also lost its character as a pragmatist actor. It does not have the power to adapt or bounce forward in a context of turmoil. Less acute crises in the neighbourhood also demand less flexibility, selective engagement, short-term action, even fewer shared responsibilities. The need to mediate conflict management goals and nationally determined priorities disappears, mainly because the member states are less interested in an EU role in crisis management. In a world of power rivalry and weakened EU, the capacity for enhancing relations has ebbed away. EUFSP is also less elastic and flexible given the inability of EU institutions to centralise or at least coordinate action across different policy areas.

If member states unanimously agree, the Union is still able to exert significant economic and diplomatic power and carry out some of the crisis and conflict management activities it performs currently. Although to a significantly lesser extent than in the two scenarios seen above, in this one too the EU remains an amplifier of the international influence of its members. However, this would result from contingent factors (member states agreeing unanimously over an extended period of time over goals and means to address a crisis or conflict) and not structural ones. Besides, the value that a fractured EU adds to member states' foreign policies is modest. A fractured EU has such a limited actorness in international security that it can barely be defined as a collective actor any longer. The Union has become an ancillary framework for the foreign and security policy of EU countries (Figure 5.1).

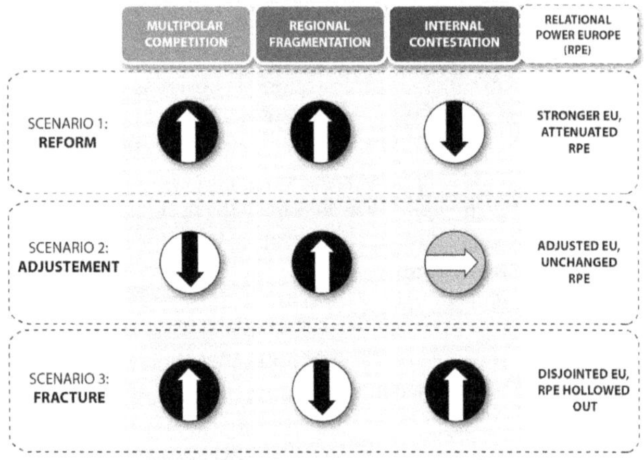

Figure 5.1. Three scenarios for Relational Power Europe. Courtesy of Oriol Farrés.

Conclusion

In this chapter, we have tested the validity of the concept of relational power to describe the EU's actorness in futures in which different combinations of contextual factors result in more or less integrated EUFSP structures.

Undoubtedly the systemic element with the greatest impact on the ability of member states to reduce the level of domestic contestation is geopolitical competition and specifically the way in which the United States engages in it. In our scenarios, an America that focuses on Asia but remains politically and strategically connected to a Europe grappling with a persistently fragmented neighbourhood spurs the strengthening of EUFSP structures. Conversely, an America that sees its relationship with Europe almost exclusively through the prism of its primacy-driven contest with China and other powers generates disaggregating dynamics within the Union. The degree of regional fragmentation in a context of more intense geopolitical competition is less indicative of whether EU states would opt for stronger or weaker cooperation. We have speculated that lower levels of fragmentation disincentivise integrated approaches, as well as the need for urgent and responsive action. By the same token, a high degree of regional fragmentation in a context of relatively contained multipolar competition may bring about a moderate strengthening of EUFSP structures.

Our three scenarios of reform, adjustment and fracture of EUFSP structures are compatible with these configurations of contextual factors, but they could also result from other combinations. For instance, a disjointed EU could result from an entirely endogenous process of rising Euroscepticism and nationalism, although we believe disaggregation presupposes a strong degree of US disengagement from Europe anyway. At any rate, what most matters to us is not to determine which combination of factors produces which scenario of integration (there are several combinations that can produce similar scenarios). Instead, our intent is to assess the sustainability of the concept of relational power depending on the greater or lesser ability of the EU and its member states to handle contextual challenges.

In this sense, the result of our analysis is clear. The Union remains a relational power in a reform scenario as much as in an adjustment scenario, albeit with a different distribution of weight between the two elements that constitute the relationality of the EUFSP: dependence on context and resilience to contextual challenges. In a more integrated

Union the relational nature of EUFSP is attenuated because the stronger resilience to the contextual factors lowers the EU's reliance on others to achieve its foreign and security policy objectives. In an adjusted Union, the constitutive dependence on context of EUFSP remains as pervasive as it is today, while the EU's reliance on internal synergies and extensive engagements, both of which are more contingent than structural, is unchanged. Instead, the concept of relational power loses its salience in a fractured Union, since the EU's ability to enhance relationships within itself and with third actors has all but vanished.

Notes

1 For a similar foresight exercise see Marianne Riddervold, Jarle Trondal and Akasemi Newsome (eds), *The Palgrave Handbook of EU Crises*, Cham, Palgrave Macmillan, 2021.

2 Davide Angelucci et al., "Public Opinion and the European Foreign and Security Policy: Is There a Risk of Politicisation?", in *JOINT Research Papers*, No. 25, April 2024, https://www.jointproject.eu/?p=2067.

3 Former German Chancellor Angela Merkel well summarised the sentiment in 2018 when she admitted publicly that the EU could no longer rely on the "superpower of the United States". See "Merkel Says Europe Can't Rely on U.S. to Impose World Order", in *Reuters*, 20 July 2018, https://www.reuters.com/article/idUSKBN1KA1F9.

4 The foreign policy literature on the point is growing. For an overview, see the fall 2023 special issue of *Internationale Politik Quarterly* (https://ip-quarterly.com/en/node/39291) and in particular Nathalie Tocci, "The Enlargement and Reform Conundrum", in *Internationale Politik Quarterly*, No. 4/2023, fall 2023, https://ip-quarterly.com/en/enlargement-and-reform-conundrum.

5 European Council, *Council Conclusions* (EUCO 20/23), 15 December 2023, https://www.consilium.europa.eu/media/68967/europeancouncil-conclusions-14–15-12-2023-en.pdf.

6 Leonardo Puleo, "Summary of Party Positions on EU Foreign, Security and Defence Policy. Case Studies: France, Germany, Greece, Italy, Poland and Spain", in *JOINT Research Papers*, No. 9, June 2022, https://www.jointproject.eu/?p=1066.

7 Conference on the Future of Europe, *Report on the Final Outcome: May 2022*, Brussels, Publications Office of the EU, 2022, in particular pp. 64–67, https://data.europa.eu/doi/10.2860/637445.

8 The report came out in September: Olivier Costa and Daniela Schwarzer (rapporteurs), *Sailing on High Seas: Reforming and Enlarging the EU for the 21st Century*, Report of Franco-German Working Group on EU Institutional Reform, Paris and Berlin, 18 September 2023, https://institutdelors.eu/en/?p=152994.

9 Belgium et al., *Joint Statement of the Foreign Ministries on the Launch of the Group of Friends on Qualified Majority Voting in EU Common Foreign*

and Security Policy, 4 May 2023, https://www.auswaertiges-amt.de/en/newsroom/news/-/2595304.

10 Enrico Letta, *Much More than a Market. Speed, Security, Solidarity*, April 2024, https://www.consilium.europa.eu/media/ny3j24sm/much-more-than-a-market-report-by-enrico-letta.pdf. Draghi explicitly called for a "radical change" of the EU: see Mario Draghi, *The Future of European Competitiveness*, September 2024, https://commission.europa.eu/document/download/97e481fd-2dc3–412d-be4c-f152a8232961_en?filename=The%20future%20of%20European%20competitiveness%20_%20A%20competitiveness%20strategy%20for%20Europe.pdf; see also Draghi, *Radical Change—Is What Is Needed*, Speech at the High-level Conference on the European Pillar of Social Rights, Brussels, 16 April 2024, https://geopolitique.eu/en/?p=16702.

11 Pierangelo Isernia et al., "Inventory of EUFSP-Related Public and Elite Opinion Surveys", in *JOINT Research Papers*, No. 10, June 2022, https://www.jointproject.eu/?p=1103.

12 Rossella Borri et al., "European Public Opinion on the Challenges and Future of EU Foreign and Security Policy", in *JOINT Research Papers*, No. 23, January 2024, https://www.jointproject.eu/?p=1936.

13 Non-paper by Bulgaria, Croatia, the Czech Republic, Denmark, Estonia, Finland, Latvia, Lithuania, Malta, Poland, Romania, Slovenia, and Sweden on the outcome of and follow-up to the Conference on the Future of Europe, 9 May 2022. The statement was disseminated, amongst others, through the X\Twitter account of Sweden's Permanent Representation to the EU: https://twitter.com/SwedeninEU/status/1523637827686531072/photo/1.

14 Davide Angelucci et al., "Public Opinion and the European Foreign and Security Policy: Is There a Risk of Politicisation?", in *JOINT Research Papers*, No. 25, April 2024, https://www.jointproject.eu/?p=2067

15 Davide Angelucci et al., "Public Opinion and the European Foreign and Security Policy: Is There a Risk of Politicisation?", in *JOINT Research Papers*, No. 25, April 2024, https://www.jointproject.eu/?p=2067

16 Rossella Borri et al., "European Public Opinion on the Challenges and Future of EU Foreign and Security Policy", in *JOINT Research Papers*, No. 23, January 2024, https://www.jointproject.eu/?p=1936.

17 Rossella Borri et al., "European Public Opinion on the Challenges and Future of EU Foreign and Security Policy", in *JOINT Research Papers*, No. 23, January 2024, https://www.jointproject.eu/?p=1936.

18 Rossella Borri et al., "European Public Opinion on the Challenges and Future of EU Foreign and Security Policy", in *JOINT Research Papers*, No. 23, January 2024, https://www.jointproject.eu/?p=1936.

19 Thomas Christiansen, "The EU's New Normal: Consolidating European Integration in an Era of Populism and Geo-Economics", *Journal of Common Market Studies*, Vol. 58, Annual Review, 2020, pp. 13–27, https://doi.org/10.1111/jcms.13106.

20 We have built our scenarios based on existing literature, our own knowledge and intense exchanges with colleagues with expertise in each of the various policy domains considered. We would like to thank our colleagues from IAI

Luca Barana, Margherita Bianchi, Matteo Bonomi, Ettore Greco, Alessandro Marrone and Nathalie Tocci.

21 For more details about the "staged accession" option, see Milena Mihajlović et al., *Template 2.0 for Staged Accession to the EU*, Brussels, Centre for European Policy Studies and Open Society Foundation, August 2023, https://www.ceps.eu/?p=40577.

22 Such a reformed EU could, for instance, provide Ukraine with more sustainable flows of military shipments as well as with more sophisticated weapon systems. It could also deploy military assets in conflict areas with stabilisation goals; for example, the deployment of a robust CSDP mission to Libya in the second half of the 2010s could have secured the UN-supported government in Tripoli and pushed back against spoilers such as Russia and Egypt (while also making Turkey's involvement less appealing for the Libyan government).

23 To make one example: it is highly unlikely, if not impossible altogether, that the Council would use QMV to force decisions on Kosovo that the five non-recognising states would find unacceptable. For an overview of the general reluctance of EU member states to outvote others, see Paul Bochtler et al., *EU Council Monitor. The Use of Qualified Majority Voting in the EU Council (2010–2023)*, 19 April 2024, https://doi.org/10.18449/IV01v1.0.

24 Articles 42.5 and 44 of the Treaty on the EU gives the Council the authority entrust the implementation of certain tasks to a group of willing and able member states, who act on behalf of the Union within the limits set by the Council's mandate.

Conclusions

Europe's predicament worsened considerably in the early part of the 21st century. While the United States-China global contest loomed large on the horizon, Russia's aggressiveness upended continental security and interstate rivalries destabilised the EU's southern neighbourhood. Local conflicts in the Middle East, North Africa and the Horn of Africa transcended borders, intensifying migration flows, putting strains on economic structures, exacerbating social and political tensions, and fuelling illicit trafficking as well as the proliferation of armed militias and extremism. In parallel, the EU faced its own internal upheaval, with the Eurozone and Schengen crises as well as Brexit jolting the bedrock of intra-EU solidarity and augmenting contestation of EU policies. The combination and interplay of multipolar competition, regional fragmentation and internal contestation came to define the context against which EU and national policymakers pursued conflict and crisis management.

Against this backdrop, we have argued that the EU's actorness in international security could be fully appreciated when considered in relation to its composite context, not least because the structures presiding over EU foreign and security policy largely remained stable from the late 2000s onwards. Accordingly, we have refrained from focusing on the EU's values and normative background and institutional design and observed instead how EU institutions and member states handled the contextual challenges. We have narrowed the analytical reach of our research to crises and conflicts occurring between the mid-2000s and the early 2020s because in them the interplay between the three factors played out most visibly.

Combining an outside-in perspective with the more established inside-out ones, we have conceptualised the EU as a relational power. We contend that this concept captures both the constitutive dependence

DOI: 10.4324/9781003559467-7

on context of EU foreign and security policy and the resilience that EU institutions and member states show in handling the challenges emanating from that context. The EU acts as a vigorous diplomatic entity, proficient in initiating numerous dialogue platforms and advancing relations simultaneously on various levels: with external parties, within different policy sectors, among member states and between the latter and EU institutions. In applying our framework, we have injected some nuance into the generally negative assessment of EU foreign and security policy, widely perceived as stagnant and ineffective. In the timeframe under consideration, results were indeed below expectations due to an adverse combination of contextual factors, but EU foreign and security policy was not always ineffective and rarely stagnant. The EU was resourceful and creative in finding ways to manage conflicts and crises, despite internal and external constraints.

In managing multipolar pressures, we have found that the EU leaned more towards multilateralism than geopolitics, prioritising inclusive coalitions and engagement with international regimes over power contests. An eloquent example of this is the resolve with which the E3 and HRVP anchored the Iranian nuclear dispute to Tehran's internationally binding obligations and promoted a multilateral resolution scheme that was extended to rival countries such as the United States, on the one hand, and Russia and China, on the other. The EU also promoted an International Contact Group on Venezuela, built a dialogue with some ASEAN countries with the aim of strengthening the legal framework for the settlement of territorial disputes in the South China Sea, supported the initial UN-led multilateral efforts to manage the civil wars in Syria and Libya, and through the Franco-German duo tried to resolve the conflict in the Donbas by negotiating with Russia and relying on the Organisation for Security and Cooperation in Europe.

While the EU pursued multilateralisation of crisis and conflict management efforts, it always remained fastened in the Euro-Atlantic order centred on the United States. The EU regularly pursued transatlantic convergence as a pillar of its inclusive multilateralism and defence of a rules-based order, especially the ad hoc multilateralism carried out by crisis formats such as contact groups. Again, the Iran case is emblematic. The E3/EU leveraged the multilateral group that also included China and Russia to facilitate US-Iranian nuclear engagement in a multilateral and normative framework rather than a geopolitical one shaped by brute force. A similar approach, albeit with decidedly modest results, was adopted with regard to Venezuela, although initially the Americans pursued a regime change objective that the Europeans, keener on national reconciliation, did not entirely share; and Syria, where however transatlantic collaboration (and more at the bilateral member states level than at the EU level) soon turned towards fighting ISIS rather than conflict resolution. At times, transatlantic collaboration was minimal and not really supportive of multilateral solutions (these are the cases of Israel-Palestine and Ukraine pre-2022). When the multilateral option was impossible to exercise, the EU fell back on the strategic partnership with the United States, as the coordinated response to the second Russian invasion of Ukraine in 2022 attests.

We have also observed how the EU's approach to managing regional fragmentation reflected its elasticity and pragmatism. An example of effective selective and pragmatist engagement is again offered by the Iran case, where the prioritisation of the nuclear issue and its consequent compartmentalisation from other concerns regarding the Islamic Republic in the region allowed the E3 and HRVP to give an essential contribution to the process that led to the 2015 nuclear deal. Another example was the decoupling of Kosovo's final status from the management of EU relations with Serbia and Kosovo itself, which advanced over the years even if the conflict remained unsolved.

The pragmatism behind selective engagement was more often a reflection of the inability of the EU and its member states to interact with conflict actors on a higher political level. Relatively positive experiences in this regard span the EU's capacity-building partnerships with a few ASEAN countries in the South China Sea and the combination of humanitarian aid and election monitoring in Venezuela. By contrast, EU assistance to the Palestinian Authority's security and border control forces had no real impact on the conflict with Israel. At other times, selective engagement was the result of an inability to reconcile divergent priorities, as was the case in Libya.

We have further observed how, despite the cacophony of voices in EU foreign policy debates, deeper harmonies persisted, allowing member states to overcome divisions and function as a collective, albeit non-homogeneous, actor. When deliberation and negotiation, the standard procedures for overcoming intra-EU disagreements, failed, the EU was at times still able to produce substantive policy through both direct delegation to common institutions or indirect delegation to lead groups. The EU would have had much more trouble managing relations with Kosovo if the five member states that do not recognise its independence had been called upon to play a leading role instead of being able to hide behind the HRVP and the Commission. Similarly, the EU could hardly have played the role that it finally did on the Iranian nuclear issue, had it not been for the original initiative of the E3. Further, it is because Germany and France joined forces in an attempt to find a resolution to the conflict in the Donbas that the EU was able to play a conflict management role there, however secondary (and eventually unsuccessful) it was.

In sum, we have found that a relational power Europe resorted to multiple strategies, tactics and practices in the process of handling the deep and mutually reinforcing systemic constraints and their interaction with European domestic politics. In conflict management, this resulted in an EU that is instinctively multilateralist, strategically Atlanticist and structurally incapable of engaging in sustained geopolitical contests alone; an EU that is more elastic, favouring inclusivity and secondary issues and more pragmatist (some would say cynical) than normative when addressing conflicts in areas of fragmentation. This is an EU that manages to be more than the sum of its parts in more instances than the unanimity rule would allow for at first sight, but still does so on an ad hoc rather than systemic basis.

These conclusions – the EU as a partly multilateralist, partly Atlanticist, pragmatist and polymorphic actor – are hardly revolutionary. The point for us was not so much to come up with new attributes of EU foreign and security policy, but to show how these features ultimately result from the EU's *modus operandi* in crisis and conflict management, which is all about mitigating the constraining action of the contextual factors. In this sense, we have complemented the theoretical perspectives that draw from norms and institutions when conceptualising the EU's actorness in international security as a normative or civilian power, a "quiet" great power or a small one, a green or regulatory power, and so on. In addition, our perspective allows us to contrast the empirical reality with the self-representations that the EU constructed in a series of strategic documents since the early 2000s. Neither "effective multilateralism" (as in the ESS), nor "principled pragmatism" (as in the EUGS) nor "geopolitical power" (as in most recent documents and statements) are accurate descriptions of the organising principles of EU foreign and security policy, although we have observed that elements of each contribute to shaping the EU's actorness.

The relational nature of EU foreign and security policy can be detected in other international players that are affected by similar contextual dynamics and therefore react to their negative effects. In these terms, it may be difficult to distinguish the EU from a sovereign state endowed with limited resources and located in a difficult international predicament. A state can be equally multilateralist and Atlanticist, as well as pragmatist and extremely flexible in its interactions with actors operating in fragmented areas. In this sense, the definition of relational power creates a correspondence between the EU in international security and a second-order state actor. The Union behaves not so much as a 'power' but as a state that must rely on variable multilateral engagements – now more inclusive and cooperative, now more exclusive and confrontational – depending on circumstances that it cannot control.

However, the relational nature of its foreign and security policy reflects something absolutely specific to the EU, namely its nature as a supranational-intergovernmental hybrid, which for once is a strength rather than a weakness, as it is a source of greater resilience. More than states and other international organisations, the EU builds its power on the possibility to bolster relations. Its inherent structure facilitates dialogue and engages with regional institutions, while its multilateral nature establishes it as a credible interlocutor for conflict or crisis parties. At the same time, the EU functions as a geopolitically aligned collective actor, utilising well-established mechanisms for collaboration with allied countries, most notably the United States. The EUFSP's multi-sectoral structure allows for asymmetrical interventions with varying focus, size and scope. Moreover, its multi-actor character enables policy formulation, initiation and implementation from multiple points within the Union, sustaining efforts despite internal differences and contestation. In this sense, when we speak of a relational power Europe, we speak of an entity that offers possibilities for action that would otherwise be precluded to its member states. The relational power of the EU is about handling the contextual challenges by mobilising all elements making up its multi-dimensional foreign and security policy structures.

Our review of how relational power Europe acted in a series of crises and conflicts has shown that in some cases the EU managed to gain larger margins for action, sometimes so considerable as to make it a first-rate player. But it has also revealed that there are severe limitations to relational power Europe. The EU was often reduced to little more than a secondary player whose policy had modest if not insignificant effects, and sometimes it was counterproductive. Even in the successful cases, relational power Europe achieved only provisional results susceptible to reversal when the interweaving of contextual factors became more intense, as attested to by the collapse of the Iran nuclear deal following the United States' withdrawal from it or the failure of the Normandy framework to persuade Russia to renounce its imperial designs. We infer from this that EU member states may well soon be tempted – if they are not already – to pursue their security interests *collectively* only in a *reformed EU* or *individually* in a *fractured one*. Relational power Europe can be seen as too dependent on contextual factors and on the possibility to enhance relations with others, which are sometimes difficult to sustain.

Both reform and fragmentation of EUFSP are plausible options, even though they point in opposite directions. There is no doubt that the never-abated inner demand for continuous integration has become louder due to outer pressures, from the Russian threat to Middle Eastern instability to uncertainties in the Indo-Pacific, as well as the possibility of a US disengagement from Europe. Yet the interplay of these systemic factors with the domestic politics of the member states does not provide any certain indication about whether the future will see more integration, less integration or even disaggregation in foreign, security and defence policy. In fact, that interplay creates a space that political entrepreneurs both for and against further integration can occupy to bring public opinion to their side. Still, we assume that stronger multipolar competition is likelier to result in a more integrated EU if the United States sees the transatlantic relationship as politically and strategically valuable per se. In contrast, a United States that sees it exclusively through the prism of a primacy-driven contest with China would more probably fuel intra-EU contestation and EUFSP dis-articulation. At any rate, we conclude this book not with a prediction but rather a reflection on the future applicability of our concept of relational power Europe.

This concept will undoubtedly continue to be meaningful in a scenario of sectoral adjustment of the EUFSP's institutional set-up because the EU will be permeated by contextual factors, constrained by the persistence of multipolar competition and regional fragmentation, but also resilient to them. Yet the challenge of an 'adjusted EU', a relational power Europe which draws its power from its capacity to sustain relations, will be to hold on to the term 'power' in a world dominated by hard security and geopolitical competition. A 'fractured EU', however, would be much less able to engage in the relationships that underpin the concept of relational power, which would therefore lose its analytical grip. Instead, a 'reformed EU' would lead to a recalibration of the concept of relational power Europe, since the impact of the context on the constitution of the EU's actorness in international security would be attenuated by the greater EUFSP assets the Union would gain. However, 'less' does not mean 'not at all'; whatever degree of integration the EU may realistically attain, as long as its nature as a supranational-intergovernmental hybrid and multi-actor, multi-sector system remains, the interplay between the external world and the domestic politics of the member states will continue to define its actorness in international security.

References

Mohamed Ali Abdolgader, "Turkey, and Iran: Why Rival Powers Are Backing Ethiopia's Government", in *The New Arab*, 14 February 2022, https://www.newarab.com/node/1289463

Amitav Acharya, "After Liberal Hegemony: The Advent of a Multiplex World Order", in *Ethics & International Affairs*, Vol. 31, No. 3 (2017), pp. 271–285, https://doi.org/10.1017/S089267941700020X

Amitav Acharya, *The End of American World Order*, 2nd ed., Cambridge/Medford, Polity Press, 2018.

Cornelius Adebahr, *Europe and Iran. The Nuclear Deal and Beyond*, London/New York, Routledge, 2017.

Rebecca Adler-Nissen and Vincent Pouliot, "Power in Practice: Negotiating the International Intervention in Libya", in *European Journal of International Relations*, Vol. 20, No. 4 (2014), pp. 889–911, https://doi.org/10.1177/1354066113512702

Christer Ahlström, "The EU Strategy against Proliferation of Weapons of Mass Destruction", in Shannon N. Kile (ed.), *Europe and Iran. Perspectives on Non-proliferation*, Oxford, Oxford University Press, 2005, pp. 27–46, https://www.sipri.org/node/1633

Jesutimilehin O. Akamo, Caterina Bedin and Dario Cristiani, "The Vicious Circle of Fragmentation: The EU and the Limits of Its Approach to Libya", in *JOINT Research Papers*, No. 15 (February 2023), https://www.jointproject.eu/?p=1521

Sinem Akgül-Açıkmeşe and Soli Özel, "EU Policy towards the Israel-Palestine Conflict: The Limitations of Mitigation Strategies", in *The International Spectator*, Vol. 59, No. 1 (2024), pp. 59–78, https://doi.org/10.1080/03932729.2024.2309664

Riccardo Alcaro, *Europe and Iran's Nuclear Crisis. Lead Groups and EU Foreign Policymaking*, Cham, Palgrave Macmillan, 2018.

Riccardo Alcaro (ed.), *The Liberal Order and Its Contestations. Great Powers and Regions Transiting in a Multipolar Era*, London/New York, Routledge, 2018.

Riccardo Alcaro, "Europe's Defence of the Iran Nuclear Deal: Less than a Success, More than a Failure", in *The International Spectator*, Vol. 56, No. 1 (2021), pp. 55–72, https://doi.org/10.1080/03932729.2021.1876861

Riccardo Alcaro, "Weathering the Geopolitical Storms: The Ever-elusive Success of EU Policy towards Iran", in *The International Spectator*, Vol. 59, No. 1 (2024), pp. 98–119, https://doi.org/10.1080/03932729.2023.2273852

Riccardo Alcaro and Hylke Dijkstra, "Re-imagining EU Foreign and Security Policy in a Complex and Contested World", in *The International Spectator*, Vol. 59, No. 1 (2024), pp. 1–18, https://doi.org/10.1080/03932729.2024.2304028

Riccardo Alcaro and Marco Siddi, "Lead Groups in EU Foreign Policy: The Cases of Iran and Ukraine", in *European Review of International Studies*, Vol. 8, No. 2 (2021), pp. 143–165, https://doi.org/10.1163/21967415-08020016

Riccardo Alcaro and Nathalie Tocci, "Navigating a Covid World: The art. 47's Internal Rebirth and External Quest", in *The International Spectator*, Vol. 56, No. 2 (2021), pp. 1–18, https://doi.org/10.1080/03932729.2021.1911128

Riccardo Alcaro, John Peterson and Ettore Greco (eds), *The West and the Global Power Shift. Transatlantic Relations and Global Governance*, Basingstoke/New York, Palgrave Macmillan, 2016.

Paula Alvarez-Couceiro, "Europe at a Strategic Disadvantage: A Fragmented Defense Industry", in *War on the Rocks*, 18 April 2023, https://warontherocks.com/?p=28598

Maria Giulia Amadio Viceré and Monika Sus, "Differentiated Cooperation as the Mode of Governance in EU Foreign Policy", in *Contemporary Security Policy*, Vol. 44, No. 1 (2023), pp. 4–34, https://doi.org/10.1080/13523260.2023.2168854

Davide Angelucci, Pierangelo Isernia, Carlotta Mingardi, Francesco Olmastroni, "Public Opinion and the European Foreign and Security Policy: Is there a Risk of Politicisation?", in *JOINT Research Papers*, No. 25 (April 2024), https://www.jointproject.eu/?p=2067

Suzana Anghel, "Strategic Sovereignty for Europe", in *EPRS Briefings*, September 2020, https://www.europarl.europa.eu/thinktank/en/document/EPRS_BRI(2020)652069

Rosanne Anholt and Giulia Sinatti, "Under the Guise of Resilience: The EU Approach to Migration and Forced Displacement in Jordan and Lebanon", in *Contemporary Security Policy*, Vol. 41, No. 2 (2020), pp. 311–335, https://doi.org/10.1080/13523260.2019.1698182

Ioannis Armakolas and James Ker-Lindsay (eds), *The Politics of Recognition and Engagement. EU Member State Relations with Kosovo*, Cham, Palgrave Macmillan, 2020.

Anna Ayuso, Marianne Riddervold and Elsa Lilja Gunnarsdottir, "The EU Trapped in the Venezuelan Labyrinth: Challenges to Finding a Way Out", in *JOINT Research Papers*, No. 18 (February 2023), https://www.jointproject.eu/?p=1550

Anna Ayuso et al., “Constraints, Dilemmas and Challenges for EU Foreign Policy in Venezuela”, in *The International Spectator*, Vol. 59, No. 1 (2024), pp. 140–160, https://doi.org/10.1080/03932729.2023.2289647

Alyson J.K. Bailes, “The European Security Strategy. An Evolutionary History”, in *SIPRI Policy Papers*, No. 10 (February 2005), https://www.sipri.org/node/1631

Kristin M. Bakke, Kathleen Gallagher Cunningham and Lee J.M. Seymour, “A Plague of Initials: Fragmentation, Cohesion, and Infighting in Civil Wars”, in *Perspectives on Politics*, Vol. 10, No. 2 (2012), pp. 265–283, https://doi.org/10.1017/S1537592712000667

Rosa Balfour (ed.), *Europe's Troublemakers. The Populist Challenge to Foreign Policy*, Brussels, European Policy Centre, 2016, https://www.epc.eu/en/Publications/~257da8

Elena Baracani, “Evaluating EU Actorness as a State-Builder in ‘Contested’ Kosovo”, in *Geopolitics*, Vol. 25, No. 2 (2020), pp. 362–386, https://doi.org/10.1080/14650045.2018.1563890

Esther Barbé and Pol Morillas, “The EU Global Strategy: The Dynamics of a More Politicized and Politically Integrated Foreign Policy”, in *Cambridge Review of International Affairs*, Vol. 32, No. 6 (2019), pp. 753–770, https://doi.org/10.1080/09557571.2019.1588227

Pol Bargués, “From ‘Resilience’ to Strategic Autonomy: A Shift in the Implementation of the Global Strategy?”, in *EU-LISTCO Policy Papers*, No. 9 (February 2021), https://zenodo.org/doi/10.5281/zenodo.4548132

Pol Bargués, “Peacebuilding without Peace? On How Pragmatism Complicates the Practice of International Intervention”, in *Review of International Studies*, Vol. 46, No. 2 (2021), pp. 237–255, https://doi.org/10.1017/S0260210520000042

Pol Bargués, Assem Dandashly, Hylke Dijkstra and Gergana Noutcheva, “Engagement against All Odds? Navigating Member States’ Contestation of EU Policy on Kosovo”, in *The International Spectator*, Vol. 59, No. 1 (2024), pp. 19–38, https://doi.org/10.1080/03932729.2023.2295893

Pol Bargués, Assem Dandashly, Hylke Dijkstra and Gergana Noutcheva, “Time to Re-engage with Kosovo and Serbia: Strengthening EU Foreign and Security Policy amidst Internal Contestation”, in *JOINT Research Papers*, No. 12 (December 2022), https://www.jointproject.eu/?p=1459

Pol Bargués, Jonathan Joseph and Ana E. Juncos, “Rescuing the Liberal International Order: Crisis, Resilience and EU Security Policy”, in *International Affairs*, Vol. 99, No. 6 (2023), pp. 2281–2299, https://doi.org/10.1093/ia/iiad222

Julien Barnes-Dacey and Daniel Levy, “Making the Most of Geneva II”, in *ECFR Commentaries*, 17 January 2014, https://ecfr.eu/?p=5377

Douglas Barrie, Ben Barry, Henry Boyd, Nick Childs and Bastian Giegerich, “Europe’s Defence Requires Offence”, in *Survival*, Vol. 63, No. 1 (2021), pp. 19–24, https://doi.org/10.1080/00396338.2021.1881249

Aniseh Bassiri Tabrizi and Benjamin Kienzle, "The High Representative and *Directoires* in European Foreign Policy: The Case of the Nuclear Negotiations with Iran", in *European Security*, Vol. 29, No. 3 (2020), pp. 320–336, https://doi.org/10.1080/09662839.2020.1798407

Caterina Bedin, Tiffany Guendouz and Agnès Levallois, "From Conflict Management to Shielding EU Stability: How Syria's Fragmentation Diverted the EU(FSP) from Action to Reaction", in *The International Spectator*, Vol. 59, No. 1 (2024), pp. 79–97, https://doi.org/10.1080/03932729.2023.2277212

Belgium, Finland, France, Germany, Italy, Luxembourg, Netherlands, Slovenia, Spain, *Joint Statement of the Foreign Ministries on the Launch of the Group of Friends on Qualified Majority Voting in EU Common Foreign and Security Policy*, 4 May 2023, https://www.auswaertiges-amt.de/en/newsroom/news/-/2595304

Max Bergman, "Europe Needs a Paradigm Shift in How It Supports Ukraine", in *CSIS Commentaries*, 17 January 2024, https://www.csis.org/node/108942

Max Bergman and Sophia Besch, "Why European Defense Still Depends on America", in *Foreign Affairs*, 7 March 2023, https://www.foreignaffairs.com/node/1130056

Federica Bicchi, "'Our Size Fits All': Normative Power Europe and the Mediterranean", in *Journal of European Public Policy*, Vol 13, No. 2 (2006), pp. 286–303, https://doi.org/10.1080/13501760500451733

Christopher J. Bickerton, Dermot Hodson and Uwe Puetter, "The New Intergovernmentalism: European Integration in the Post-Maastricht Era", in *Journal of Common Market Studies,* Vol. 53, No. 4 (2014), pp. 703–722, https://doi.org/10.1111/jcms.12212

Katja Biedenkopf, Oriol Costa and Magdalena Góra, "Introduction: Shades of Contestation and Politicisation of CFSP", in *European Security*, Vol. 30, No. 3 (2021), pp. 325–343, https://doi.org/10.1080/09662839.2021.1964473

Sven Biscop, "No Peace from Corona: Defining EU Strategy for the 2020s", in *Journal of European Integration*, Vol. 42, No. 8 (2020), pp. 1009–1023, https://doi.org/10.1080/07036337.2020.1852230

Steven Blockmans, "The Birth of a Geopolitical EU", in *European Foreign Affairs Review*, Vol. 27, No. 2 (2022), pp. 155–160, https://doi.org/10.54648/eerr2022016

Paul Bochtler et al., *EU Council Monitor. The Use of Qualified Majority Voting in the EU Council (2010-2023)*, 19 April 2024, https://doi.org/10.18449/IV01v1.0

Josep Borrell, "Embracing Europe's Power", in *Project Syndicate*, 8 February 2020, https://prosyn.org/UZNbi12

Josep Borrell, "Europe in the Interregnum: Our Geopolitical Awakening after Ukraine", in *Géopolitique*, 24 March 2022, https://geopolitique.eu/en/?p=10796

Rossella Borri et al., "European Public Opinion on the Challenges and Future of EU Foreign and Security Policy", in *JOINT Research Papers*, No. 23 (January 2024), https://www.jointproject.eu/?p=1936

Tanja A. Börzel and Thomas Risse, *Effective Governance Under Anarchy. Institutions, Legitimacy, and Social Trust in Areas of Limited Statehood*, Cambridge, Cambridge University Press, 2021.

Dimitris Bouris, *The European Union and Occupied Palestinian Territories. State Building without a State*, London/New York, Routledge, 2014.

Anu Bradford, *The Brussels Effect. How the European Union Rules the World*, Oxford/New York, Oxford University Press, 2020.

Mats Braun, "Postfunctionalism, Identity and the Visegrad Group", in *Journal of Common Market Studies*, Vol. 58, No. 4 (2020), pp. 925–940, https://doi.org/10.1111/jcms.12994

Ian Bremmer, *Every Nation for Itself. Winners and Losers in a G-Zero World*, London, Portfolio/Penguin, 2012.

Stephen G. Brooks and William C. Wohlforth, "The Myth of Multipolarity", in *Foreign Affairs*, Vol. 102, No. 3 (May/June 2023), pp. 76–91.

Bulgaria, Croatia, the Czech Republic, Denmark, Estonia, Finland, Latvia, Lithuania, Malta, Poland, Romania, Slovenia, and Sweden, *Non-paper by Bulgaria, Croatia, the Czech Republic, Denmark, Estonia, Finland, Latvia, Lithuania, Malta, Poland, Romania, Slovenia, and Sweden on the outcome of and follow-up to the Conference on the Future of Europe*, 9 May 2022, https://twitter.com/SwedeninEU/status/1523637827686531072/photo/1

Hedley Bull, "Civilian Power Europe: A Contradiction in Terms?", in *Journal of Common Market Studies*, Vol. 21, No. 2 (1982), pp. 149–170, https://doi.org/10.1111/j.1468-5965.1982.tb00866.x

Barry Buzan, "How Regions Were Made, and the Legacies for World Politics: An English School Reconnaissance", in T. V. Paul (ed.), *International Relations Theory and Regional Transformation*, Cambridge, Cambridge University Press 2012, pp. 22–46.

David Cadier and Christian Lequesne, "How Populism Impacts EU Foreign Policy", in *EU-LISTCO Policy Papers*, No. 8 (November 2020), https://zenodo.org/doi/10.5281/zenodo.4282192

Thanassis Cambanis et al. (eds), *Hybrid Actors. Armed Groups and State Fragmentation in the Middle East*, New York, The Century Foundation Press, 2019, https://tcf.org/content/report/hybrid-actors

Francesca Caruso and Jesutimilehin Akamo, "EU Policy towards Ethiopia amidst the Tigray War: The Limits of Mitigating Fragmentation", in *The International Spectator*, Vol. 59, No. 1 (2024), pp. 120–139, https://doi.org/10.1080/03932729.2024.2302473

Michela Ceccorulli and Fabrizio Coticchia, "'I'll Take Two.' Migration, Terrorism, and the Italian Military Engagement in Niger and Libya", in *Journal of Modern Italian Studies*, Vol. 25, No. 2 (2020), pp. 174–196, https://doi.org/10.1080/1354571X.2020.1723291

Thomas Christiansen, "The EU's New Normal: Consolidating European Integration in an Era of Populism and Geo-Economics", in *Journal of Common*

Market Studies, Vol. 58, Annual Review (September 2020), pp. 13–27, https://doi.org/10.1111/jcms.13106

Christopher Coker, *The Rise of the Civilizational State*, Cambridge/Medford, Polity Press, 2019.

Conference on the Future of Europe, *Report on the Final Outcome: May 2022,* Brussels, Publications Office of the EU, 2022, https://data.europa.eu/doi/10.2860/637445

Eugenia da Conceição-Heldt and Sophie Meunier, "Speaking with a Single Voice: Internal Cohesiveness and External Effectiveness of the EU in Global Governance", in *Journal of European Public Policy*, Vol. 21, No. 7 (2014), pp. 961–979, https://doi.org/10.1080/13501763.2014.913219

Oriol Costa and Esther Barbé, "A Moving Target. EU Actorness and the Russian Invasion of Ukraine", in *Journal of European Integration*, Vol. 45, No. 3 (2023), pp. 431–446, https://doi.org/10.1080/07036337.2023.2183394

Olivier Costa and Daniela Schwarzer (rapporteurs), *Sailing on High Seas: Reforming and Enlarging the EU for the 21st Century*, Report of Franco-German Working Group on EU Institutional Reform, Paris and Berlin, 18 September 2023, https://institutdelors.eu/en/?p=152994

Council of the EU, *European Security Strategy. A Secure Europe in a Better World*, Brussels, Publications Office of the EU, 2009, https://data.europa.eu/doi/10.2860/1402

Council of the EU, *Council Conclusions on the Integrated Approach to External Conflicts and Crises* (5413/18), 22 January 2018, https://data.consilium.europa.eu/doc/document/ST-5413-2018-INIT/en/pdf

Council of the EU, *Terms of Reference of an International Contact Group on Venezuela*, 30 January 2019, https://www.consilium.europa.eu/media/38043/st05958-en19-icg-terms-of-reference.pdf

Council of the EU, Council Decision (CFSP) 2021/509 of 22 March 2021 *Establishing a European Peace Facility*, https://data.europa.eu/eli/dec/2021/509/2024-03-18

Council of the EU, *A Strategic Compass for Security and Defence*, 14 March 2022, https://www.eeas.europa.eu/node/410976_en

Tarja Cronberg, "No EU, No Iran Deal: The EU's Choice between Multilateralism and the Transatlantic Link", in *The Nonproliferation Review*, Vol. 24, No. 3–4 (2017), pp. 243–259, https://doi.org/10.1080/10736700.2018.1432321

Kathleen Cunningham, "Understanding Fragmentation in Conflict and its Impact on Prospects for Peace", in *Oslo Forum Papers*, No. 6 (December 2016), https://hdcentre.org/?p=17920

Chad Damro, "Market Power Europe", in *Journal of European Public Policy*, Vol. 19, No. 5 (2012), pp. 682–699, https://doi.org/10.1080/13501763.2011.646779

Cedric De Coning and Mateja Peter, *United Nations Peace Operations in a Changing Global Order*, Cham, Palgrave Macmillan, 2019, https://doi.org/10.1007/978-3-319-99106-1

Philip de Man, Gustavo Müller and Andriy Tyushka, "Proposals to Improve the EU's Engagement in Conflict Resolution, Prevention and Mediation", in *ENGAGE Working Papers*, No. 14 (November 2022), https://www.engage-eu.eu/publications/the-eus-engagement-in-conflict-resolution-prevention-and-mediation

Pieter de Wilde and Hans J. Trenz, "Denouncing European Integration: Euroscepticism as Polity Contestation", in *European Journal of Social Theory*, Vol. 15, No. 4 (2012), pp. 537–554, https://doi.org/10.1177/1368431011432968

Raffaella A. Del Sarto, "Normative Empire Europe: The European Union, Its Borderlands, and the 'Arab Spring'", in *Journal of Common Market Studies*, Vol. 54, No. 2 (2016), pp. 215–232, https://doi.org/10.1111/jcms.12282

Sandra Destradi, David Cadier and Johannes Plagemann, "Populism and Foreign Policy: A Research Agenda (Introduction)", in *Comparative European Politics*, Vol. 19, No. 6 (2021), pp. 663–682, https://doi.org/10.1057/s41295-021-00255-4

Desmond Dinan, Neill Nugent and William E. Paterson (eds), *The European Union in Crisis*, London, Palgrave, 2017.

Mario Draghi, *Radical Change—Is What Is Needed*, Speech at the High-level Conference on the European Pillar of Social Rights, Brussels, 16 April 2024, https://geopolitique.eu/en/?p=16702

Mario Draghi, *The future of European competitiveness*, September 2024, https://commission.europa.eu/document/download/97e481fd-2dc3-412d-be4c-f152a8232961_en?filename=The%20future%20of%20European%20competitiveness%20_%20A%20competitiveness%20strategy%20for%20Europe.pdf

Francois Duchêne, "Europe's Role in World Peace", in Richard Mayne (ed.), *Europe Tomorrow. Sixteen Europeans Look Ahead*, London, Fontana, 1972, pp. 32–47.

François Duchêne, "The European Community and the Uncertainties of Interdependence", in Max Kohnstamm and Wolfgang Hager (eds), *A Nation Writ-Large? Foreign-Policy Problems before the European Community*, London/Basingstoke, Macmillan, 1973, pp. 1–21.

Bruno Dupré, "European Sovereignty, Strategic Autonomy, Europe as a Power: What Reality for the European Union and for What Future?", in *Schuman Papers*, No. 620 (25 January 2022), https://www.robert-schuman.eu/en/european-issues/0620

Joanna Dyduch, "The Visegrád Group's Policy towards Israel", in *SWP Comments*, No. 54 (December 2018), https://www.swp-berlin.org/en/publication/the-visegrad-groups-policy-towards-israel

Joanna Dyduch and Patrick Müller, "Populism Meets EU Foreign Policy: The De-Europeanization of Poland's Foreign Policy toward the Israeli-Palestinian Conflict", in *Journal of European Integration*, Vol. 43, No. 5, (2021), pp. 569–586, https://doi.org/10.1080/07036337.2021.1927010

Michael Emerson and Steven Blockman, The $300 Billion Question – How to Get Russia to Pay for Ukraine's Reconstruction, in *SCEEUS Guest Platform for Eastern Europe Policy*, No 4 (14 December 2022), https://www.ceps.eu/?p=38555

Dina Esfandiary and Ariane Tabatabai, *Triple-Axis. Iran's Relations with Russia and China*, London/New York, I.B. Tauris, 2021.

European Commission, *The EU Approach to Resilience: Learning from Food Security Crises* (COM 2012/586), 3 October 2012, https://eur-lex.europa.eu/legal-content/en/TXT/?uri=celex:52012DC0586

European Commission, *Action Plan for Resilience in Crisis Prone Countries 2013-2020* (SWD 2013/227), 19 June 2013, https://aei.pitt.edu/58235

European Commission and EEAS, *A Strategic Approach to Resilience in the EU's External Action* (JOIN 2017/21), 7 June 2017, https://eur-lex.europa.eu/legal-content/en/TXT/?uri=celex:52017JC0021

European Commission, *Speech by President-elect von der Leyen in the European Parliament Plenary on the Occasion of the Presentation of her College of Commissioners and Their Programme*, 27 November 2019, https://ec.europa.eu/commission/presscorner/detail/en/speech_19_6408

European Commission, *State of the Union 2023*, 13 September 2023, https://ec.europa.eu/commission/presscorner/detail/en/speech_23_4426

European Council, *Council Conclusions* (EUCO 20/23), 15 December 2023, https://www.consilium.europa.eu/media/68967/europeancouncilconclusions-14-15-12-2023-en.pdf

European External Action Service (EEAS), *Shared Vision, Common Action: A Stronger Europe. A Global Strategy for the European Union's Foreign and Security Policy*, Brussels, Publications Office of the EU, 2016, https://data.europa.eu/doi/10.2871/9875

European External Action Service (EEAS), *Annual Progress Report on the Implementation of the Strategic Compass for Security and Defence*, March 2023, https://www.eeas.europa.eu/node/426781_en

European External Action Service (EEAS), *Geopolitical Europe: Speech by High Representative/Vice-President at the EP Plenary*, 18 October 2023, https://www.eeas.europa.eu/node/434503_en

Deborah Feldman, "Germany Is a Good Place to Be Jewish. Unless, Like Me, You're a Jew Who Criticises Israel", in *The Guardian*, 13 November 2023, https://www.theguardian.com/p/paj6c

Daniel Fiott, "In Every Crisis an Opportunity? European Union Integration in Defence and the War on Ukraine", in *Journal of European Integration*, Vol. 45, No. 3 (2023), pp. 447–462, https://doi.org/10.1080/07036337.2023.2183395

Alexander Gabuev, "Russia's Support for Venezuela Has Deep Roots", in *Financial Times*, 3 February 2019, https://www.ft.com/content/0e9618e4-23c8-11e9-b20d-5376ca5216eb

Ivan Garcia, "The Future of the Sino-Venezuelan Relationship: Make or Break?", in *Harvard International Review*, 22 December 2021, https://hir.harvard.edu/the-future-of-the-sino-venezuelan-relationship-make-or-break

Philipp Genschel, Lauren Leek and Jordy Weyns, "War and Integration. The Russian Attack on Ukraine and the Institutional Development of the EU", in *Journal of European Integration*, Vol. 45, No. 3 (2023), pp. 345–360, https://doi.org/10.1080/07036337.2023.2183397

Josip Glaurdić, *The Hour of Europe. Western Powers and the Breakup of Yugoslavia*, New Haven/London, Yale University Press, 2011.

Arancha González Laya et al., "*Trump-Proofing Europe*", in *Foreign Affairs*, 24 February 2024, https://www.foreignaffairs.com/node/1131310

Nicole Grajewski, "The Evolution of Russian and Iranian Cooperation in Syria", in *CSIS Analyses*, November 2021, https://www.csis.org/node/63071

Susanne Gratius, "The West Against the Rest? Democracy Versus Autocracy Promotion in Venezuela", in *Bulletin of Latin American Research*, Vol. 41, No. 1 (2022), pp. 141–58, https://doi.org/10.1111/blar.13243

Roberta Guerrina and Katharine A.M. Wright, "Gendering Normative Power Europe: Lessons of the Women, Peace and Security Agenda", in *International Affairs*, Vol. 92, No. 2 (2016), pp. 293–312, https://doi.org/10.1111/1468-2346.12555

Montserrat Guibernau, "The Birth of a United Europe: on Why the EU Has Generated a 'Non-Emotional' Identity", in *Nations and Nationalism*, Vol. 17, No. 2 (2011), pp. 302–315, https://doi.org/10.1111/j.1469-8129.2010.00477.x

Jorge Guzmán and Mónica Rico Benitez, "A New Role for the EU in Venezuela", in *CEPS Expert Opinions*, 4 December 2020, https://www.ceps.eu/?p=31515

Maria Gwynn, "Structural Power and International Regimes", in *Journal of Political Power*, Vol. 12, No. 2, (2019), pp. 200–223.

Richard N. Haass, "The Age of Nonpolarity", in *Foreign Affairs*, Vol. 87, No. 3 (May/June 2008), pp. 44–56. https://www.foreignaffairs.com/articles/united-states/2008-05-03/age-nonpolarity

Calle Håkansson, "The Ukraine War and the Emergence of the European Commission as a Geopolitical Actor", in *Journal of European Integration*, Vol. 46, No. 1 (2024), pp. 25–45, https://doi.org/10.1080/07036337.2023.2239998

Peo Hansen and Stefan Johnson, *Eurafrica: The Untold Story of European Integration and Colonialism*, London, Bloomsbury, 2014.

Sebastian Harnisch, "Minilateral Cooperation and Transatlantic Coalition-Building", in *European Security*, Vol. 16, No. 1 (2007), pp. 1–27, https://doi.org/10.1080/09662830701442261

Pierre Haroche, "A 'Geopolitical Commission': Supranationalism Meets Global Power Competition", in *Journal of Common Market Studies*, Vol. 61, No. 4 (2023), pp. 970–987, https://doi.org/10.1111/jcms.13440

Graeme P. Herd (ed.), *Great Powers and Strategic Stability in the 21st Century. Competing Visions of World Order*, London/New York, Routledge, 2010.

Anna Herranz-Surralles, "The EU Energy Transition in a Geopoliticizing World", in *Geopolitics*, Vol. 29, No. 5 (2024), pp. 1882–1912, https://doi.org/10.1080/14650045.2023.2283489

Christopher Hill, "The Capability-Expectations Gap: Or Conceptualising Europe's International Role", in *Journal of Common Market Studies*, Vol. 31, No. 3 (1993), pp. 305–328, https://doi.org/10.1111/j.1468-5965.1993.tb00466.x

Christopher Hill, "Convergence, Divergence and Dialectics: National Foreign Policies and the CFSP", in Jan Zielonka (ed.), in *Paradoxes of European Foreign Policy*, The Hague, Kluwer Law International, 1998, pp. 35–51.

Liesbet Hooghe and Gary Marks, "A Postfunctionalist Theory of European Integration: From Permissive Consensus to Constraining Dissensus", in *British Journal of Political Science*, Vol. 39, No. 1 (2009), pp. 1–23, https://doi.org/10.1017/S0007123408000409

Liesbeth Hooghe and Gary Marks, "Grand Theories of European Integration in the Twenty-First Century", in *Journal of European Public Policy*, Vol. 26, No. 8 (2019), pp. 1113–1133, https://doi.org/10.1080/13501763.2019.1569711

Jolyon Howorth, "The EU's Chair Was Missing at the Ukraine Table", *European View*, Vol. 21, No. 1, (2022), pp. 27–35, https://journals.sagepub.com/doi/full/10.1177/17816858221089371.

Adrian Hyde-Price, *Germany and European Order. Enlarging NATO and the EU*, Manchester/New York, Manchester University Press, 2000.

Adrian Hyde-Price, "'Normative' Power Europe: A Realist Critique", in *Journal of European Public Policy*, Vol. 13, No. 2 (2006), pp. 217–234, https://doi.org/10.1080/13501760500451634

International Commission on the Balkans, *The Balkans in Europe's Future*, Sofia: Bosch Stiftung, King Badouin Foundation, German Marshall Fund of the United States, Stewart Mott Foundation, 2005.

International Crisis Group, "Realigning European Policy toward Palestine with Ground Realities", in *Middle East Reports*, No. 237 (23 August 2022), https://www.crisisgroup.org/node/19491

International Crisis Group, "Is Restoring the Iran Nuclear Deal Still Possible?", in *Middle East & North Africa Briefings*, No. 87 (12 September 2022), https://www.crisisgroup.org/node/19560

Pierangelo Isernia, Francesco Olmastroni, Rossella Borri, Carlotta Mingardi, "Inventory of EUFSP-related Public and Elite Opinion Surveys", in *JOINT Research Papers*, No. 10 (June 2022), https://www.jointproject.eu/?p=1103

Anna Jarstad, Johanna Söderström and Malin Åkebo, *Relational Peace Practices*, Manchester, Manchester University Press, 2023.

Rosa Jiménez, "Borrell: la misión de observación electoral de la UE hizo avanzar la democracia venezolana", in *EuroEFE Euroactiv*, 26 January 2022, https://euroefe.euractiv.es/?p=55141

Ana E. Juncos, "Resilience as the New EU Foreign Policy Paradigm: A Pragmatist Turn?", in *European Security*, Vol. 26, No. 1 (2017), pp. 1–18, https://doi.org/10.1080/09662839.2016.1247809

Ana E. Juncos and Steven Blockmans, "The EU's Role in Conflict Prevention and Peacebuilding: Four Key Challenges", in *Global Affairs*, Vol. 4, No. 2–3 (2018), pp. 131–140, https://doi.org/10.1080/23340460.2018.1502619

Ana E. Juncos and Karolina Pomorska, "Contesting Procedural Norms: The Impact of Politicisation on European Foreign Policy Cooperation", in *European Security*, Vol. 30. No. 3 (2021), pp. 367–384, https://doi.org/10.1080/09662839.2021.1947799

Ana E. Juncos and Simon Frankel Pratt, "Pragmatist Power Europe: Resilience and Evolution in Planetary Organic Crisis", in *Cooperation and Conflict*, 22 April 2024, https://doi.org/10.1177/00108367241244958

Kristina Kausch, "Competitive Multipolarity in the Middle East", in *The International Spectator*, Vol. 50, No. 3 (2015), pp. 1–15, https://doi.org/10.1080/03932729.2015.1055927

Kristina Kausch, "A Decade of Deadlock. The EU's Shipwreck on Palestine Embodies the EU's Blockade Problem", in *JOINT Briefs*, No. 33 (March 2024), https://www.jointproject.eu/?p=2011

Bilahari Kausikan, "The Arena", in *Foreign Affairs,* Vol. 100, No. 2 (March/April 2021), pp. 186–191.

Stephan Keukeleire and Sharon Lecocq, "Operationalising the Decentring Agenda: Analysing European Foreign Policy in a Non-European and Post-Western World", in *Cooperation and Conflict*, Vol. 53, No. 2, 2018, pp. 277–295.

Kiel Institute for the World Economy, *Ukraine Support Tracker*, updated on 16 February 2024, https://www.ifw-kiel.de/topics/war-against-ukraine/ukraine-support-tracker

Zelal Başak Kizilkan, "Changing Policies of Turkey and the EU to the Syrian Conflict", in *Journal of Economics and Administrative Sciences*, Vol. 33, No. 1 (2019), pp. 321–338, https://dergipark.org.tr/en/pub/atauniiibd/issue/43125/457846

Mareike Kleine and Mark Pollack, "Liberal Intergovernmentalism and Its Critics", in *Journal of Common Market Studies*, Vol. 56, No. 7 (2018), pp. 1493–1509, https://doi.org/10.1111/jcms.12803

Stephan Klingebiel, Timo Mahn and Mario Negre, "Fragmentation: A Key Concept for Development Cooperation", in Stephan Klingebiel, Timo Mahn and Mario Negre (eds), *The Fragmentation of Aid. Concepts, Measurements and Implications for Development Cooperation*, London, Palgrave Macmillan, 2016, pp. 1–18.

Theresa Kuhn, "Grand Theories of European Integration Revisited: Does Identity Politics Shape the Course of European Integration?", in *Journal of European Public Policy*, Vol. 26, No. 8 (2019), pp. 1213–1230, https://doi.org/10.1080/13501763.2019.1622588

Charles A. Kupchan, *No One's World. The West, the Rising Rest, and the Coming Global Turn*, Oxford/New York, Oxford University Press, 2012.

Milja Kurki, "Relational Revolution and Relationality in IR: New Conversations", in *Review of International Studies*, Vol. 48, No. 5, 2022, p. 824.

Wolfram Lacher, *Libya's Fragmentation. Structure and Process in Violent Conflict*, London, I.B. Tauris, 2020.

Brigid Laffan, "Collective Power Europe? (The Government and Opposition/Leonard Schapiro Lecture 2022)", in *Government and Opposition*, Vol. 58, No. 4 (2023), pp. 623–640, https://doi.org/10.1017/gov.2022.52

Zaki Laïdi, "Towards a Post-Hegemonic World: The Multipolar Threat to the Multilateral Order", in *International Politics*, Vol. 51, No. 3 (2014), pp. 350–365, https://doi.org/10.1057/ip.2014.13

Christian Lamour, "Orbán Placed in Europe: Ukraine, Russia and the Radical-Right Populist Heartland", in *Geopolitics*, Vol. 29, No. 4 (2023), pp. 1297–1323. https://doi.org/10.1080/14650045.2023.2241825

Sandra Lavenex and Marija-Liisa Öberg, "Third Country Influence on EU Law and Policymaking: Setting the Scene", in *Journal of Common Market Studies*, Vol. 61, No. 6, (2023), pp. 1435–1453.

Andrew Lebovich and Tarek Megerisi, "France's Strongman Strategy in the Sahel", in *ECFR Commentaries*, 8 March 2019, https://ecfr.eu/?p=8011

Mark Leonard, *The Age of Unpeace. How Connectivity Causes Conflict*, London, Penguin Random House/Bantam, 2021.

Mark Leonard, "The European Union as a War Project. Five Pathways toward a Geopolitical Europe", in Hal Brands (ed.), *War in Ukraine. Conflict, Strategy, and the Return of a Fractured World*, Baltimore, Johns Hopkins University Press, 2024, pp. 258–272, https://muse.jhu.edu/pub/1/oa_edited_volume/chapter/3881930

Enrico Letta, *Much More than a Market. Speed, Security, Solidarity*, April 2024, https://www.consilium.europa.eu/media/ny3j24sm/much-more-than-a-market-report-by-enrico-letta.pdf

Agnès Levallois et al., "Regional Fragmentation and EU Foreign and Security Policy", in *JOINT Research Papers*, No. 3 (November 2021), https://www.jointproject.eu/?p=639

Debbie Lisle, "A Speculative Lexicon of Entanglement", in *Millennium*, Vol. 49, No. 3 (2021), pp. 435–461, https://doi.org/10.1177/03058298211021919

Andrew Lohsen and Pierre Morcos, "Understanding the Normandy Format and Its Relation to the Current Standoff with Russia", in *CSIS Critical Questions*, 9 February 2022, https://www.csis.org/node/63952

Marianna Lovato et al., "The Internal Contestation of EU Foreign and Security Policy", in *JOINT Research Papers*, No. 1 (September 2021), https://www.jointproject.eu/?p=516

Alexander Lukin, *Russia and China. The New Rapprochement*, Cambridge, Polity Press, 2018.

Aron Lund, "Helping Syria without Helping Assad: A Zero-Sum Game for Brussels?", in Francesco Salesio Schiavi (ed.), "Aid and Diplomacy: The EU Donors' Conference for Syria and Türkiye", in *MED This Week*, 24 March 2023, https://www.ispionline.it/en?p=122328

Anna-Sophie Maass, "The Actorness of the EU's State-Building in Ukraine – Before and after Crimea", in *Geopolitics*, Vol. 25, No. 2 (2020), pp. 387–406, https://doi.org/10.1080/14650045.2018.1559149

Ian Manners, "Normative Power Europe: A Contradiction in Terms?", in *Journal of Common Market Studies*, Vol. 40, No. 2 (2002), pp. 235–258, https://doi.org/10.1111/1468-5965.00353

Alessandro Marrone (ed.), *Russia-Ukraine War's Strategic Implications*, Rome, IAI, February 2024, https://www.iai.it/en/node/18118

Heidi Maurer, Richard G. Whitman and Nicholas Wright, "The EU and the Invasion of Ukraine: A Collective Responsibility to Act?", in *International* Affairs, Vol. 99, No. 1 (2023), pp. 219–238, https://doi.org/10.1093/ia/iiac262

Heidi Maurer and Nicholas Wright, "Still Governing in the Shadows? Member States and the Political and Security Committee in the Post-Lisbon EU Foreign Policy Architecture", in *Journal of Common Market Studies*, Vol. 59, No. 4 (2021), pp. 856–872, https://doi.org/10.1111/jcms.13134

Tarek Megerisi, "Libya's Global Civil War", in *ECFR Policy Briefs*, June 2019, https://ecfr.eu/?p=4456

Hugo Meijer and Stephen G. Brooks, "Illusions of Autonomy: Why Europe Cannot Provide for Its Security If the United States Pulls Back", in *International Security*, Vol. 45, No. 4 (2021), pp. 7–43, https://doi.org/10.1162/isec_a_00405

Alessia Melcangi and Karim Mezran, "Truly a Proxy War? Militias, Institutions and External Actors in Libya between Limited Statehood and Rentier State", *The International Spectator*, Vol. 57, No. 4, (2022), pp. 121–138, https://www.tandfonline.com/doi/full/10.1080/03932729.2022.2061225

Sophie Meunier and Kalypso Nicolaïdis, "The Geopoliticization of European Trade and Investment Policy", in *Journal of Common Market Studies*, Vol. 57, Annual Review (2019), pp. 103–113, https://doi.org/10.1111/jcms.12932

Milena Mihajlović et al., *Template 2.0 for Staged Accession to the EU*, Brussels, Centre for European Policy Studies and Open Society Foundation, August 2023, https://www.ceps.eu/?p=40577

Arta Moeini, "America: The Last Ideological Empire", in *Compact Magazine*, 8 July 2022 https://www.compactmag.com/article/america-the-last-ideological-empire/

Nuno P. Monteiro, "World Order across the End of the Cold War", in Nuno P. Monteiro and Fritz Bartel (eds), *Before and After the Fall. World Politics and the End of the Cold War*, Cambridge, Cambridge University Press, 2021, pp. 338–360.

Andrew Moravcsik, "Preferences and Power in the European Community: A Liberal Intergovernmentalist Approach", in *Journal of Common Market Studies*, Vol. 31, No. 4 (1993), pp. 473–524, https://doi.org/10.1111/j.1468-5965.1993.tb00477.x

Andrew Moravcsik, "Europe: The Quiet Superpower", in *French Politics*, Vol. 7, No. 3-4 (2009), pp. 403–422, https://doi.org/10.1057/fp.2009.29

Andrew Moravcsik, "Preferences, Power and Institutions in 21st-Century Europe", in *Journal of Common Market Studies*, Vol. 56, No. 7 (2018), pp. 1648–1674, https://doi.org/10.1111/jcms.12804

Pol Morillas, *Strategy-Making in the EU. From Foreign and Security Policy to External Action*, Cham, Palgrave Macmillan, 2019.

Pol Morillas, "Autonomy in Intergovernmentalism: The Role of de Novo Bodies in External Action during the Making of the EU Global Strategy", in *Journal of European Integration*, Vol. 42, No. 2 (2020), pp. 231–246, https://doi.org/10.1080/07036337.2019.1666116

Patrick Müller and David Gazsi, "Populist Capture of Foreign Policy Institutions: The Orbán Government and the De-Europeanization of Hungarian Foreign Policy", in *Journal of Common Market Studies*, Vol. 61, No. 2 (2023), pp. 397–415, https://doi.org/10.1111/jcms.13377

Patrick Müller, Karolina Pomorska and Ben Tonra, "The Domestic Challenge to EU Foreign Policymaking: From Europeanisation to de-Europeanisation?", in *Journal of European Integration*, Vol. 43, No. 5 (2021), pp. 519–534, https://doi.org/10.1080/07036337.2021.1927015

Michal Natorski and Karolina Pomorska, "Trust and Decision-making in Times of Crisis: The EU's Response to the Events in Ukraine", in *Journal of Common Market Studies*, Vol. 55, No. 1 (2017), pp. 54–70, https://doi.org/10.1111/jcms.12445

Marek Newman (ed.), *Democracy Promotion and the Normative Power Europe Framework. The European Union in South Eastern Europe, Eastern Europe, and Central Asia*, Cham, Springer, 2019.

Arne Niemann, *Explaining Decisions in the European Union*, Cambridge, Cambridge University Press, 2006.

Arne Niemann, "Neofunctionalism", in Marianne Riddervold, Jarle Trondal and Akasemi Newsome (eds), *The Palgrave Handbook of EU Crises*, Cham, Palgrave Macmillan, 2021, pp. 115–133.

Mitchell A. Orenstein, "The European Union's Transformation after Russia's Attack on Ukraine", in *Journal of European Integration*, Vol. 45, No. 3 (2023), pp. 333–342, https://doi.org/10.1080/07036337.2023.2183393

Adrian Pabst, *Liberal World Order and Its Critics. Civilisational States and Cultural Commonwealths*, London/New York, Routledge, 2019.

Michelle Pace, Peter Seeberg and Francesco Cavatorta, "The EU's Democratization Agenda in the Mediterranean: A Critical Inside-Out Approach", in *Democratization*, Vol. 16, No. 1 (2009), pp. 3–19, https://doi.org/10.1080/13510340802575783

Zachary Paikin, "Great Power Rivalry and the Weakening of Collective Hegemony: Revisiting the Relationship between International Society and International Order", in *Cambridge Review of International Affairs*, Vol. 34, No. 1 (2021), pp. 22–45, https://doi.org/10.1080/09557571.2020.1720602

Zachary Paikin, "Multipolar Competition and the Rules-based Order: Probing the Limits of EU Foreign and Security Policy in the South China Sea", in *The International Spectator*, Vol. 59 No. 1 (2024), pp. 161–178, https://doi.org/10.1080/03932729.2023.2280598

Zachary Paikin, Ilke Toygür, Martin Quencez, Stephen R. Nagy, "The Rise of Mega-Regions Eurasia, the Indo-Pacific, and the Transatlantic Alliance in a Reshaped World Order", in *CEPS In-depth Analysis*, November 2022, https://www.ceps.eu/?p=38396

Franziska Petri, Elodie Thevenin and Lins Liedlbauer, "Contestation of European Union Foreign Policy: Causes, Modes and Effects", in *Global Affairs*, Vol. 6, No. 4–5 (2020), pp. 323–328, https://doi.org/10.1080/23340460.2020.1863159

Christopher Phillips, "The Civil War in Syria: The Variety of Opposition to the Syrian Regime", in *IEMed Mediterranean Yearbook 2013*, pp. 24–29, https://www.iemed.org/publication/the-civil-war-in-syria-the-variety-of-opposition-to-the-syrian-regime

Marc Pierini, "In Search of an EU Role in the Syrian War", in *Carnegie Reports*, August 2016, https://carnegieendowment.org/publications/64352

Uwe Puetter, *The European Council and the Council. New Intergovernmentalism and Institutional Change*, Oxford, Oxford University Press, 2014.

Uwe Puetter and Sergio Fabbrini, "Catalysts of Integration – The Role of Core Intergovernmental Forums in EU Politics", in *Journal of European Integration*, Vol. 38, No. 5 (2016), pp. 633–642, https://doi.org/10.1080/07036337.2016.1179294

Giulio Pugliese, "The European Union's Security Intervention in the Indo-Pacific: Between Multilateralism and Mercantile Interests", in *Journal of Intervention and Statebuilding*, Vol. 17, No. 1 (2023), pp. 76–98, https://doi.org/10.1080/17502977.2022.2118425

Leonardo Puleo, "Summary of Party Positions on EU Foreign, Security and Defence Policy. Case Studies: France, Germany, Greece, Italy, Poland and Spain", in *JOINT Research Papers*, No. 9 (June 2022), https://www.jointproject.eu/?p=1066

Kristi Raik, Kristine Berzina, Ivo Juurvee, Tony Lawrence, Maurice Turner, "Not Yet Fit for the World: Piecemeal Buildup of EU Military, Cyber and Intelligence Assets", in *JOINT Research Papers*, No. 4 (November 2021), https://www.jointproject.eu/?p=648

Kristi Raik, Steven Blockmans, Anna Osypchuk and Anton Suslov, "EU Policy towards Ukraine: Entering Geopolitical Competition over European Order", in *The International Spectator*, Vol. 59, No. 1 (2024), pp. 39–58, https://doi.org/10.1080/03932729.2023.2296576

Jason Ralph, *On Global Learning. Pragmatic Constructivism, International Practice and the Challenge of Global Governance*, Cambridge, Cambridge University Press, 2023.

Marianne Riddervold, Jarle Trondal and Akasemi Newsome (eds), *The Palgrave Handbook of EU Crises*, Cham, Palgrave Macmillan, 2021.

Pernille Rieker and Mathilde Tomine Eriksdatter Giske, "Conceptualising the Multi-Actor Character of EU(rope)'s Foreign Policy", in *JOINT Research Papers*, No. 2 (October 2021), https://www.jointproject.eu/?p=538

Pernille Rieker and Mathilde Tomine Eriksdatter Giske, *European Actorness in a Shifting Geopolitical Order. European Strategic Autonomy Through Differentiated Integration*, Cham, Palgrave Macmillan, 2024, https://doi.org/10.1007/978-3-031-44546-0

Thomas Risse, "Social Constructivism and European Integration", in Antje Wiener and Thomas Diez (eds), *European Integration Theory*, 2nd ed., New York, Oxford University Press, 2009, pp. 144–160.

Scott Ritter, *Dealbreaker. Donald Trump and the Unmaking of the Iran Nuclear Deal*, Atlanta, GA, Clarity Press, 2018.

Robert I. Rotberg (ed.), *When States Fail. Causes and Consequences*, Princeton, Princeton University Press, 2004.

Sten Rynning, "The False Promise of Continental Concert: Russia, the West and the Necessary Balance of Power", in *International Affairs*, Vol. 91, No. 3 (2015), pp. 539–552, https://doi.org/10.1111/1468-2346.12285

Beken Saatçioğlu, "The EU's Response to the Syrian Refugee Crisis: A Battleground among Many Europes", in *European Politics and Society*, Vol. 22, No. 5 (2021), pp. 808–823, https://doi.org/10.1080/23745118.2020.1842693

Frank Schimmelfennig, "European Integration (Theory) in Times of Crisis. A Comparison of the Euro and Schengen Crises", in *Journal of European Public Policy*, Vol. 25, No. 7 (2018), pp. 969–989, https://doi.org/10.1080/13501763.2017.1421252

Frank Schimmelfennig, "The Advent of Geopolitical Enlargement and Its Credibility Dilemma", in Jelena Džankić, Simonida Kacarska and Soeren Keil (eds), *A Year Later. War in Ukraine and Western Balkan (Geo)Politics*, Brussels, Publications Office of the EU, 2023, pp. 185–193, https://data.europa.eu/doi/10.2870/275946

Leonard Schuette and Hylke Dijkstra, "The Show Must Go On: The EU's Quest to Sustain Multilateral Institutions since 2016", in *Journal of Common Market Studies*, Vol. 61, No. 5 (2023), pp. 1318–1336, https://doi.org/10.1111/jcms.13466

Simon Schunz, Sieglinde Gstöhl and Luk Van Langenhove, "Between Cooperation and Competition: Major Powers in Shared Neighbourhoods", in *Contemporary Politics*, Vol. 24, No. 1 (2018), pp. 1–13, https://doi.org/10.1080/13569775.2017.1408174

Christoph Schwegmann, "The Contact Group and Its Impact on the European Institutional Structure", in *EUISS Occasional Papers*, No. 16 (2000), https://www.iss.europa.eu/node/103

Mathieu Segers and Steven van Hecke (eds), *The Cambridge History of the European Union: Volume 1, European Integration Outside-In*, Cambridge, Cambridge University Press, 2023.

Mathieu Segers and Steven Van Hecke, *The Cambridge History of the European Union: Volume 2, European Integration Inside-Out*, Cambridge University Press, 2023.

Lucia A. Seybert and Peter J. Katzenstein, "Protean Power and Control Power: Conceptual Analysis", in Peter J. Katzenstein and Lucia A. Seybert (eds), *Protean Power. Exploring the Uncertain and Unexpected in World Politics*, Cambridge, Cambridge University Press, 2018, pp. 3–26.

Joshua Shanes, "Netanyahu, Orbán, and the Resurgence of Antisemitism: Lessons of the Last Century", in *Shofar*, Vol. 37, No. 1 (2019), pp. 108–120, https://doi.org/10.5703/shofar.37.1.0108

Marco Siddi, Tyyne Karjalainen and Juha Jukela, "Differentiated Cooperation in the EU's Foreign and Security Policy: Effectiveness, Accountability, Legitimacy", in *The International Spectator*, Vol. 57, No. 1 (2022), pp. 107–123, https://doi.org/10.1080/03932729.2022.2026683

Luis Simón, "Europe, the Rise of Asia and the Future of the Transatlantic Relationship", in *International Security*, Vol. 91, No. 5 (2015), pp. 969–989, https://doi.org/10.1111/1468-2346.12393

Luis Simón, Daniel Fiott and Octavian Manea, *Two Fronts, One Goal. Euro-Atlantic Security in the Indo-Pacific Age*, The Marathon Initiative, August 2023, https://themarathoninitiative.org/wp-content/uploads/2023/08/Two-Fronts-One-Goal-website-publication-v.2.pdf

Helene Sjursen, "What Kind of Power?", in *Journal of European Public Policy*, Vol. 13, No. 2 (2006), pp. 169–181, https://doi.org/10.1080/13501760500451584

Sandrino Smeets, Alenka Jaschke and Derek Beach, "The Role of the EU Institutions in Establishing the European Stability Mechanism: Institutional Leadership under a Veil of Intergovernmentalism", in *Journal of Common Market Studies*, Vol. 57, No. 4 (2019), pp. 675–691, https://doi.org/10.1111/jcms.12842

Karen E. Smith, *European Union Foreign Policy in a Changing World*, Cambridge, Polity Press, 2003.

Michael E. Smith, *Europe's Foreign and Security Policy: The Institutionalization of Cooperation*, Cambridge, Cambridge University Press, 2003.

Stelios Stavridis, "'Militarising' the EU: The Concept of Civilian Power Europe Revisited", in *The International Spectator*, Vol 36, No. 4 (2001), pp. 43–50, https://doi.org/10.1080/03932720108456945

Zeev Sternhell, "Why Benjamin Netanyahu Loves the European Far-Right", in *Foreign Policy*, 24 February 2019, https://bit.ly/2Viu1we

Eric Stollenwerk, Tanja A. Börzel and Thomas Risse, "Theorizing Resilience-Building in the EU's Neighbourhood: Introduction to the Special Issue", in *Democratization*, Vol. 28, No. 7 (2021), pp. 1219–1238, https://doi.org/10.1080/13510347.2021.1957839

Susan Strange, *The Retreat of the State: The Diffusion of Power in the World Economy*, New York, Continuum, 1996.

Oliver Stuenkel, *Post-Western World. How Emerging Powers Are Remaking Global Order*, Cambridge/Malden, Polity Press, 2016.

Monika Sus, "Supranational Entrepreneurs: The High Representative and the EU Global Strategy", in *International Affairs*, Vol. 97, No. 3 (2021), pp. 823–840, https://doi.org/10.1093/ia/iiab037

Nathalie Tocci, *Framing the EU Global Strategy. A Stronger Europe in a Fragile World*, Cham, Palgrave Macmillan, 2017.

Nathalie Tocci, "Resilience and the Role of the European Union in the World", in *Contemporary Security Policy*, Vol. 41, No. 2 (2020), pp. 176–194, https://doi.org/10.1080/13523260.2019.1640342

Nathalie Tocci, *A Green and Global Europe*, Cambridge, Polity Press, 2022.

Nathalie Tocci, "The Paradox of Europe's Defense Moment", in *Texas National Security* Review, Vol. 6, No. 1 (2022–2023), pp. 99–108, https://doi.org/10.26153/tsw/44441

Nathalie Tocci, "The Enlargement and Reform Conundrum", in *Internationale Politik Quarterly*, No. 4/2023 (2023), https://ip-quarterly.com/en/node/39275

Asle Toje, "The European Union as a Small Power, or Conceptualizing Europe's Strategic Actorness", in *Journal of European Integration*, Vol. 30, No. 2 (2008), pp. 199–215, https://doi.org/10.1080/07036330802005425

Ben Tonra and Thomas Christiansen (eds), *Rethinking European Union Foreign Policy*, Manchester, Manchester University Press, 2004.

Ignasi Torrent, *Entangled Peace. UN Peacebuilding and the Limits of a Relational World*, Lanham, Rowman & Littlefield, 2021.

Sarah van Bentum and Gregor Walter-Drop, "Unlocking EU Foreign and Security Potential: Measures to Mitigate Internal Contestation, Regional Fragmentation and Multipolar Competition", in *JOINT Research Papers*, No. 24 (February 2024), https://www.jointproject.eu/?p=1954

Sarah van Bentum et al., "How to Reduce the Impact of Internal Contestation, Regional Fragmentation and Multipolar Competition on EU Foreign and Security Policy", in *JOINT Research Papers*, No. 21 (May 2023), https://www.jointproject.eu/?p=1675

Tara Varma, "European Strategic Autonomy: The Path to a Geopolitical Europe", in *The Washington Quarterly*, Vol. 47, No. 1 (2024), pp. 65–83, https://doi.org/10.1080/0163660X.2024.2327820, https://www.tandfonline.com/doi/full/10.1080/0163660X.2024.2327820?needAccess=true

Gëzim Vizoka and John Doyle, "Neo-Functional Peace: The European Union Way of Resolving Conflicts", in *Journal of Common Market Studies*, Vol. 54, No. 4 (2016), pp. 862–867, https://doi.org/10.1111/jcms.12342

Douglas Webber, "Trends in European Political (Dis)Integration. An Analysis of Postfunctionalist and Other Explanations", in *Journal of European Public Policy*, Vol. 26, No. 8 (2019), pp. 1134–1152, https://doi.org/10.1080/13501763.2019.1576760

Alexander Wendt, *Social Theory of International Politics*, Cambridge, Cambridge University Press, 1999.

Hugh White, *The China Choice. Why We Should Share Power*, Oxford, Oxford University Press, 2013.

Richard G. Whitman (ed.), *Normative Power Europe. Empirical and Theoretical Perspectives*, Basingstoke, Palgrave Macmillan, 2011.

Claudia Wiesner, "Relations, Networks, and Entanglements: the Anthropocene as a Challenge to Modern Democratic Governance in Europe", in Corinne M. Flick (ed.), *Is the Open Society Sustainable in Case of Emergency?*, Munich, Convoco! Editions, 2024.

Anders Wivel and Ole Wæver, "The Power of Peaceful Change: The Crisis of the European Union and the Rebalancing of Europe's Regional Order", in *International Studies Review*, Vol. 20, No. 2 (2018), pp. 317–325, https://doi.org/10.1093/isr/viy027

Catherine Wolfram, Simon Johnson and Łukasz Rachel, "The Price Cap on Russian Oil Exports, Explained", in *Belfer Center Policy Briefs*, December 2022, https://www.hks.harvard.edu/node/310743

Steve Wood, "Pragmatic Power EUrope?", in *Cooperation and Conflict*, Vol. 46, No. 2 (2011), pp. 242–261, https://doi.org/10.1177/0010836711406420

Richard Youngs, *Europe's Eastern Crisis. The Geopolitics of Asymmetry*, Cambridge, Cambridge University Press, 2017.

Richard Youngs, "EU Foreign Policy and Energy Strategy: Bounded Contestation", in *Journal of European Integration*, Vol. 42, No. 1 (2020), pp. 147–162, https://doi.org/10.1080/07036337.2019.1708345

Richard Youngs, *The European Union and Global Politics*, London, Red Globe Press, 2021.

Index

Note: Page numbers followed by "n" denote endnotes.

For Product Safety Concerns and Information please contact our EU representative GPSR@taylorandfrancis.com
Taylor & Francis Verlag GmbH, Kaufingerstraße 24, 80331 München, Germany

www.ingramcontent.com/pod-product-compliance
Lightning Source LLC
LaVergne TN
LVHW010922110826
845149LV00013B/2442

* 9 7 8 1 0 3 2 9 9 9 9 0 6 *